Testimonials

A book that lifts up the idea of contributing to the greater good is exactly what we need right now. I'm honored to be part of it.

—Gregory Maguire, Ph.D.

New York Times bestselling author of *Wicked*

Having known Tom (and called him one of my dearest friends) for over twenty-five years, I've always loved his authenticity, his unique way of seeing things, and his passion for being of service—and in **It Lit a Fire***, he channels that fully. I love how he talks about the fire—what it is, how to find it, hold on to it, and use it in the way you're meant to. With an approach similar to* The Artist's Way*, this book combines timeless guidance, practical prompts, and relatable stories to help us tap into the fire that burns within. Tom is exceptionally qualified to teach how to have meaningful impact because he's done this his whole life—he knows how to get to the root of what matters most, quickly and with heart. Everyone who knows Tom knows that his approach works.*

—Sherri Shepherd

Emmy Award–winning talk show host, comedian, actress, and *New York Times* bestselling author

From the moment I met Tom, I recognized his passion to create positive change in the world. As a fellow adoptive parent, I invited him onto the board of my nonprofit, Adopt Change, and have watched him pour his energy into bringing awareness, education, and support to everyone involved in creating permanent, loving families. He brings that same integrity and drive to this book—inviting you to clarify what matters and take compassionate, practical steps forward. Read **It Lit a Fire** *not only to be illuminated, but to be moved to action.*

—Deborra-lee Furness

Actor and filmmaker; founder of Adopt Change and National Adoption Awareness Week (Australia); co-founder of Hopeland

It Lit a Fire *is a reminder that doing what's right isn't just a concept—it's a practice. Tom invites readers to slow down, consider what truly matters, and choose courageous, sustainable action that serves the greater good. The stories are honest, the prompts are practical, and the result is purpose you can carry into real life—advocating, uplifting, and leaving people and communities better than you found them. If you believe an essential element of leadership—and life—is advancing equity, dignity, and opportunity, this is a book you'll keep close and return to often.*

—Bob Rivers

Chair and CEO, Eastern Bank

It Lit a Fire *is that rare book that helps readers turn personal purpose into societal impact. At a time when we need changemakers at every level and across all sectors—people who can align values with action and sustain the work without burning out—Tom offers the playbook. I've known Tom for over a decade and have seen his approach up close: he builds trust, names what matters, and turns priorities into strategy you can execute. This book distills that same rigor and heart into guidance you can apply anywhere—from classrooms to boardrooms. If you care about making the world better in your own unique way, this is a must-read.*

—Dr. Patrick Tutwiler

Secretary of Education, Commonwealth of Massachusetts

It Lit a Fire *is a powerful guide for anyone ready to put aside the outside noise that holds them back and focus on the inner calling that pulls them forward. Tom Bourdon has created a book that feels both personal and practical—moving you from "someone should do something" to "I will do something." That shift alone is transformative. This book is not about becoming the perfect version of yourself. It is about listening to what is true, following what matters, and giving yourself permission to lead in a way that reflects your values.* **It Lit a Fire** *is the companion every changemaker needs on their journey from good intentions to meaningful impact.*

—Shelley Zalis

Founder and CEO of The Female Quotient

It Lit a Fire *is a roadmap for anyone ready to do work that matters without losing themselves in the process. Through storytelling, reflection, and practical guidance, it shows readers how to connect purpose with everyday choices—and to sustain that connection over time. The Firestarter Model (Pull, Passion, and Courage) offers a fresh and actionable framework for creating change that's both meaningful and sustainable. As someone who completely reshaped my life around my purpose, it's AWESOME that Tom created the Firestarter Model.*

—Ray Arata

Founder of The Betterman Conference and author of *Showing Up: How Men Can Become Effective Allies in the Workplace*

Reading **It Lit a Fire** *felt like being reminded of what's most real and most possible in all of us. Tom doesn't just write about purpose; he holds up a mirror to it. His words invite us back to our own courage and remind us that leading with heart is one of the bravest things we can do. This book is both an invitation and a challenge: to stay open, stay brave, and stay connected to what truly matters. In a world that's moving fast* *and wearing people down, Tom offers a way to return to ourselves and to each other with compassion and renewed purpose.*

—Jennifer Brown

Inclusive leadership pioneer and *Wall Street Journal* bestselling author of *How to Be an Inclusive Leader* and *The Shape of Change*

It Lit a Fire *is a brave and luminous invitation to live your purpose out loud. Tom Bourdon writes with clarity, courage, and a deep commitment to justice—the kind that doesn't just inspire you but calls you to act. This book is a guide, a spark, and a steady hand for anyone ready to step into their own calling.*

—Jane C. Edmonds

Trailblazing civic leader advancing workforce equity; former Massachusetts Cabinet Secretary; Babson College Vice President for Programming and Community Outreach; CEO, Jane & Company, LLC

From the very first chapter, **It Lit a Fire** *pulls you in with clarity and purpose. Tom turns decades of real, on-the-ground experience into guidance that actually moves people into action. What I love most is his ability to help you get honest about what matters, and then build the systems, habits, and momentum to bring that vision to life. This book is full of practical tools and grounded wisdom, but it also feels deeply human—like someone cheering you on as you step into your purpose. If you're ready to make your impact real and sustainable, this is the book you need.*

—Julie Castro Abrams

Managing Partner at How Women Invest and CEO of How Women Lead

It Lit a Fire *showcases Tom's authenticity, courage, and deep passion for helping others step into their purpose. This book is a powerful guide for anyone seeking to make a difference and have a positive impact on the world. The stories throughout are moving, relatable, and a beautiful reminder that we each hold a spark waiting to be lit. Don't miss this book; it just might be the spark that lights your own fire.*

—Shilpa Pherwani

Principal/CEO, Ibis Consulting Group

I met Tom more than ten years ago, and from our first conversation I felt truly heard and seen. He didn't just listen—he leaned in, asked the questions that stay with you, and gently pushed me to dig deeper into who I wanted to be and how I wanted to show up. That's Tom's gift: a rare blend of curiosity, compassion, and clarity that helps you uncover the truth you've carried all along. In **It Lit a Fire**, *he brings that same presence to every page; his voice feels like he's sitting across from you—engaged, grounded, and genuinely invested in what matters most. This book doesn't just inspire purpose; it invites you to claim it. For anyone ready to step forward with authenticity and impact, Tom offers both the spark and the steady guidance you need. I'm grateful for leaders like him and will always remember the fire he lit in me—and I'm thrilled the world now gets to experience it, too.*

—Lauren Ruotolo

Disability and Women's Health advocate, author of *Unstoppable in Stilettos*, and co-founder of We Are Invincible Organization

IT LIT A FIRE

TOM BOURDON, Ed.D

IT LIT A FIRE

Let Your Inner Spark Ignite a Change reAction

Publish Your Purpose
141 Weston Street, #155
Hartford, CT, 06141

The opinions expressed by the Author are not necessarily those held by Publish Your Purpose.

Ordering Information: Quantity sales and special discounts are available on quantity purchases by corporations, associations, and others. For details, contact info@thenextlevelimpact.com.

Senior Project Manager: Alex Loutsenko
Edited by: Connie Mayse, Lily Capstick
Cover design by: Mark Pate
Typeset by: Medlar Publishing Solutions Pvt Ltd., India

ISBN: 979-8-88797-219-0 (hardcover)
ISBN: 979-8-88797-221-3 (paperback)
ISBN: 979-8-88797-223-7 (ebook)

Library of Congress Control Number: 2025926701

First edition, April 2026.

The information contained within this book is strictly for informational purposes. The material may include information, products, or services by third parties. As such, the Author and Publisher do not assume responsibility or liability for any third-party material or opinions. The publisher is not responsible for websites (or their content) that are not owned by the publisher. Readers are advised to do their own due diligence when it comes to making decisions.

Publish Your Purpose is a hybrid publisher of nonfiction books. Our mission is to elevate the voices often excluded from traditional publishing. We intentionally seek out authors and storytellers with diverse backgrounds, life experiences, and unique perspectives to publish books that will make an impact in the world. Do you have a book idea you would like us to consider publishing? Please visit PublishYourPurpose.com for more information.

I dedicate this book to
my mother, Katherine (Kay) Bourdon.
My heart beats the way it does because of her.

Table of Contents

CHAPTER 3

— ONGOING —

CHAPTER 4

CHAPTER 5

Our Journey Begins Here

You always had the power, my dear.
You just had to learn it for yourself.
—Glinda, *The Wizard of Oz* (1939)

The Spark Moment

Thank you for picking up *It Lit a Fire.*

Chances are, you're reading this because something has sparked inside of you, and it came from somewhere important. Maybe it was a moment that shook you or a steady heat that's been rising over time. Whatever the case, the feelings stirring inside of you are undeniable.

That's your fire calling to you—asking you to pay attention, lean into it, and act.

Inner fire can have many origins—love that fuels you, loss that shapes you, injustice that angers you, creativity that energizes you, or a sense of purpose that drives you. However it shows up, it's strong and it keeps tugging at you—a reminder of just how deeply you care.

You might not even fully understand it yet, but ignoring it no longer feels like an option and hiding it from others feels wrong.

You've caught yourself thinking, "Why isn't anyone doing anything? Why aren't things changing?" And now, you're done waiting for someone else to answer those questions.

You care too much to sit back. You know, deep down, that you're meant to contribute—to show up and create change. Not out of obligation, to earn praise, or to check a box, but because it's the right thing to do.

If you recognize yourself in those words, you're in the right place.

This isn't a book for people who already have it all figured out, and it's not for the fully-formed changemakers with perfect plans. It's for anyone who feels an inner calling to help create a better world and is ready to have a role in making that happen. You're not interested in performative action. You're not here to waste time. You're here because you want to have an impact that matters.

When the Fire Finds You

You didn't ask for a fire, but it found you—a flicker you couldn't ignore. Maybe it began as a low ache, a quiet knowing, or a subtle tug, but the urgency has been growing.

You notice others who burn bright with purpose, creating real change. And lately, you've felt it yourself—that restlessness that comes when something inside is ready to ignite. You know you're meant to do more.

You may be just starting to pay attention to that internal voice, the one that keeps nudging you toward something, but you're still unclear what that something is. Or maybe you have clarity and have shared your truth with others but they don't get it. Perhaps you've begun taking action but don't feel like you're seeing the impact, or maybe you've been doing the hard work for a while and are starting to feel its weight. No matter your situation, you are welcome here.

This book is for *Firestarters*—people who answer the call to take action in order to create positive change—and for those just starting out who want to learn how to take action. For some, it becomes their day job. For others, it's separate from their vocation but still where they devote much of their time and energy. Some have a unique platform or level of influence they choose to use for good.

And for some, it's simply woven into the fabric of who they are and almost everything they do.

Wherever you are on this journey, I encourage you to release any self-judgment, and know that even the most seasoned Firestarter is still learning, growing, and finding their way forward.

You believe change is possible—and you're ready to strike the match.

A Journey of Discovery

This book isn't intended to just be something you read, but also a path you walk. It is meant to challenge you, encourage you, and help you act on what matters most to you. It's not about following someone else's map—it's about discovering your own, using the tools, stories, and insights you'll find here.

Your Guide for the Journey

I'm truly honored that you've chosen to come on this journey with me.

For more than two decades, I've worked alongside changemakers of all kinds—coaching leaders, amplifying underrepresented voices, and helping people turn their values into action. My work has connected me with brilliant and passionate individuals across universities, nonprofits, global organizations, and the entertainment industry.

Even after all this time, whether I'm teaching a course, giving a keynote, or strategizing with a leadership team, I am still (and will always be) a learner at heart—fortunate to grow as much as I guide.

Like many Firestarters, I didn't always know where my path would take me next, but writing this book has been my way of sharing what I've learned on my journey, much of that influenced by the support and stories of others who have helped light the way.

The Firestarter Model

Over time, I began to notice something: The same three forces kept showing up in the lives of people committed to having a meaningful impact in the world. Wanting a way to frame that pattern and make it practical for you as a reader, I shaped those insights into the **Firestarter Model**, the foundation for everything in this book.

Many of us have voices in our heads telling us that something outside of ourselves needs attention. Those voices might speak to us frequently about all sorts of things. But every so often, there's one particular voice that keeps coming back again and again. It gets louder. It lingers. That's the **Pull**.

Generally, we're aware of the Pull. It brings up something strong—grief, frustration, awe, hope. But even then, we don't always feel personal responsibility to act. That shift from "someone should do something" to "I've got to do something" happens when **Passion** kicks in. The wheels in your brain start turning, and you're moved from observation to vision. You begin to imagine yourself becoming part of the solution, not just naming the problem.

And yet, even when Pull and Passion are alive in us, we don't always act. That's because one more essential ingredient is needed—the third log on the fire. That's **Courage**. Without it, you're unlikely to move into Firestarter mode. You won't speak up, carve out the time, dig deep into your wallet, take the daring leap, have the Courageous conversation—you might not even be brave enough to hit "post." Fear shows up in all kinds of ways and holds us back from acknowledging the Pull or tapping into our Passion. It stops your spark from igniting a fire that is meant to burn bright.

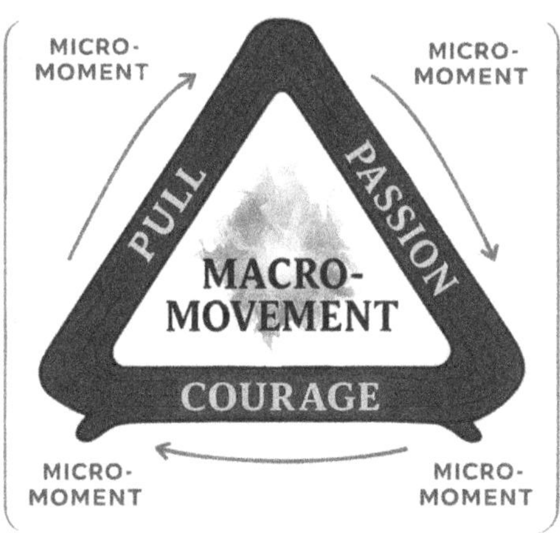

So why do some people become Firestarters, while others sit on the sidelines? Because Firestarters have been shaped by a powerful mix of micro-moments and macro-movements, both of which add fuel to the fire.

Micro-Moments are those small flashes that somehow stay with you forever. The sting from a comment someone made. The look on someone's face that you'll never forget. The story you heard that shifted everything. These moments may seem small, but their impact runs deep.

Just as powerful are the **Macro-Movements**—bigger things that have undeniably shaped you on a personal level and led to significant shifts in your life—the identity-defining experiences, the life-altering losses, the systemic injustices, the values carved into your DNA long before you could name them.

These are the elements of the Firestarter Model: Pull. Passion. Courage. Micro-Moments. Macro-Movements. Together, they create your personal roadmap for change that only *you* can follow. When combined, they may even point toward something deeper—what you might eventually come to recognize as your purpose.

My hope is that this book becomes a companion on your journey—a yellow brick road guiding you through your own growth and discovery. And just like the Scarecrow, Tin Man, and Cowardly Lion, you may question whether you have what it takes—wisdom, compassion, courage—to be a true Firestarter.

Spoiler alert: You do. You've had it all along.

Like the Scarecrow's quest for a brain, I hope you come to see that your lived experience, curiosity, and perspective are powerful forms of wisdom. Pull isn't about knowing everything—it's about trusting that inner whisper that says *it's time*.

Like the Tin Man's longing for a heart, I want you to honor the emotions that stir in you—love, pain, joy, hope. When Passion is given room to breathe, it becomes the beating center of impact.

And like the Cowardly Lion, I want you to see that Courage doesn't mean that fear has disappeared. It means you choose to move forward anyway.

You'll notice occasional *Wizard of Oz* references woven throughout the book, because its characters and metaphors align powerfully with Pull, Passion, and Courage. Just know that those three forces aren't hidden away in Emerald City—they've been inside you, waiting to be noticed, felt, and trusted. Your job is to listen to what calls you, stay close to what fuels you, and find the Courage to act.

> *When Passion is given room to breathe, it becomes the beating center of impact.*

An Opportunity to Reflect

This book will take you through the three phrases of the **Firestarter Model**: **Emerging**, **Ongoing**, and **Sustained**. Each phase includes chapters that explore what might be coming up for you in terms of **Pull**, **Passion**, and **Courage**.

You'll likely recognize parts of yourself across these phases, but reflection won't stop there. This journey invites you to consider not only where you are now, but also where you've been and where you're heading. There's value in all of it. Impact-focused journeys can pause, restart, or take unexpected turns. This book is here to honor wherever you are.

You're also going to meet incredible Firestarters in these pages—from everyday changemakers to iconic public figures from the worlds of sports, publishing, fashion, and entertainment—each sharing how Pull, Passion, and Courage have shown up and had a major influence in their own lives.

The Firestarter stories in this book were created in one of two ways: Some were drawn from written reflections shared by everyday changemakers while others came from in-depth interviews with public figures, later shaped into first-person narratives. You can even watch short video clips from select public-figure conversations through links provided at the end of each chapter.

Their stories, woven alongside my own reflections, bring the Firestarter Model to life and remind us that while impact can take countless forms, it always starts with a spark.

Each chapter closes with a series of reflective prompts to help you gain insight, clarity, and momentum on your own journey.

Before We Launch

It Lit a Fire is a blend of memoir, insights from Firestarters, personal reflections, and prompts to help you go deeper.

It is not a hero's journey where everything ties up neatly—change is messy, human, and deeply personal.

This book is for people who want to live aligned with their **values**, make a difference, and feel more alive doing it.

It is not about burning yourself out or trying to fix everything alone.

This book is an **invitation** to engage your Pull, Passion, and Courage—and to do so in a way that's sustainable, real, and uniquely *you.*

It is not about forcing action or suggesting there's only one right way forward.

This book offers a clear **framework**—the Firestarter Model—to help you reconnect with what fuels you and move forward with clarity.

It is not a business manual, leadership textbook, or motivational hype.

It's about turning that inner spark into **meaningful impact**—honoring quiet beginnings as much as bold leaps.

It is not about waiting until you have all the answers—if we did that, nothing would ever change.

From My Fire to Yours

I feel so fortunate to have been surrounded by incredible Firestarters throughout my life—driven people with huge hearts, deep values, and a fire they refuse to dim. Along with my deep admiration and gratitude, I always find myself wanting to know: Where does their fire come from? How do they decide to act on it? Why do they care so much?

This book was my way of exploring those questions while honoring the changemaking I've witnessed and the Firestarters I've met along the way. Their stories deserve to be told and uplifted, not just because they matter, but because they're powerful and inspiring. One person's spark can ignite something in someone else, and then someone else again—more sparks, more Firestarters, more impact. That's a **change reAction**.

> *One person's spark can ignite something in someone else, and then someone else again . . . That's a* ***change reAction.***

What set this book in motion was when my own Pull, Passion, and Courage aligned. Earlier this year, I had a micro-moment (which I'll share later) that created an unusually strong **Pull** to write about the fire some of us have inside. That connected directly to my longstanding **Passion** for "making this world a better place" (define as you may) and for empowering others to do the same. But this book almost didn't happen because of one thing: **Courage**. I needed to have the Courage to set aside competing priorities and write it. Courage to trust my instincts and knowledge. Courage to believe that my voice and perspective had value. Let me tell you—*all* the self-doubt came up. But rather than letting it get the best of me, I did what a true Firestarter does: I chose to put fear aside and strike the match.

We'll use the Firestarter Model throughout this book to understand the journeys of other Firestarters and spark your own reflections. I invite you to capture your insights in an Impact Journal: a space to notice patterns, track your growth, respond to prompts, and explore next steps. Scan the QR code on the next page or visit www.thenextlevelimpact.com/resources to learn more about the *It Lit a Fire* companion Impact Journal.

I hope this book gives you space to reflect on what really matters to you and helps bring focus and momentum to the change you wish to see. Some people worry they have to prove themselves before they can make an impact. If that thought has ever crossed your mind, let it go. The fact that you care deeply means you're ready to get started. You just have to listen to that inner voice and trust yourself. If this book leaves you feeling a little more inspired, a little more empowered, and just brave enough to take that next step, then it has done its job.

PART ONE

EMERGING

The First Flicker

There's a voice that doesn't use words. Listen.
—Rumi

Experience is the only thing that brings knowledge, and the longer you are on Earth the more experience you are sure to get.
—The Wizard to Scarecrow,
The Wonderful Wizard of Oz (1900)

When the Pull First Finds You

You're about to embark on a specific kind of journey—an impact journey. We'll travel it together through others' stories, my story, and yours.

Along the way, we'll explore how to create meaningful change by tapping into your inner Pull, Passion, and Courage. If it helps, picture yourself on the yellow brick road with the Scarecrow, Tin Man, and Cowardly Lion, each searching for the very qualities we'll be drawing on: wisdom (Pull), heart (Passion), and bravery (Courage). Your impact journey is about using those same qualities already *within you* to create change that matters *to you*. It's about realizing they've been there all along.

We'll be joined by others on this journey, and who better to start with than someone who's traveled the yellow brick road many times—each step guided by intention and leading to meaningful change?

You might not know the name Gregory Maguire, but chances are you've heard of *Wicked*—the novel he wrote that then became the hit Broadway musical and blockbuster movies. I met Gregory years ago, and when I began writing my book, he was one of the first people I knew I needed to talk with to better understand his story.

Yes, *Wicked* is wildly imaginative—a global phenomenon and literary masterpiece. But peel back the layers, and it's a vehicle for a powerful message that has reached millions: Don't be so quick to judge others.

As humans, our brains like to tell us we can have someone figured out in a millisecond. (Unconscious bias training, anyone?) The person who I assume I have so much in common with: friend! The neighbor with different political beliefs: foe! The Wicked Witch of the West? Obviously we don't even need a full millisecond to make that judgement call—right?

Wrong. As *Wicked* taught us, that witch wasn't who we thought she was.

As humans, we rarely get it right based on what we see on the surface. If we could all slow down just a bit—resist immediately believing what our minds are telling us—and take the time to truly get to know and understand someone (without assuming the worst), maybe this world could be a slightly better and kinder place. But how does anyone get that message out to the world?

As Gregory showed us, one way can be through story. And his impact journey didn't start with certainty—it started with a flicker and the Courage to follow his heart.

A Pull to Deeper Understanding—*Gregory Maguire*

I was 13 years old, reading the poem at the top of page 72, as directed by my Catholic school teacher. It was a short, eight-line poem. The first line was: "I'm nobody. Who are you?"

It's the start of Emily Dickinson's reflection on being fragile and isolated. "Are you nobody, too? Then there's a pair of us—don't tell! They'd banish us, you know." That poem addressed me directly. At that age, I felt like nobody. I felt incomplete, and certainly timid and insecure about who I might turn out to be.

But something happened in that moment. I realized that poetry could speak to me—and that stories had been speaking to me all along. They were a tool for communication. Where was the pull for me? It was the realization that through story I could talk to people I didn't know, and I could hear from people I would never meet.

I believe deeply that stories help us arrange meaning for ourselves. The ones that spoke to me as a child were all fairy tales, and the mothers tended to die in the first three paragraphs—leaving their undefended child to go out in the world and try to survive the wicked stepmothers and the witches and the curses.

I didn't realize at the time how much that was speaking to me in such a deep way. But I myself had a tragedy in the very first week of my life—my mother died in childbirth. I think the truth of that biography influenced the kind of stories that spoke to me as a child and therefore became the kind of stories I now rely upon as an adult.

There's something eternal about those stories. They suggest we are all alone. And we have to make our way—with grace, luck, and usually a little help—toward a satisfactory and functional adulthood. That's why fantasy, which is really just an extended fairy tale, felt like the appropriate genre for me to take up.

Story becomes a bridge—or a train—carrying meaning from a distant place to a place closer to you. It's a tool for sharing your own meaning and helping others find theirs. Stories frame things in a way we can follow, interpret, and ultimately make our own conclusions about.

And when you talk about passion—if an author can release themself, genuinely, unvarnished—the chances are that there is more live, actionable material in your work that can affect people. The more genuine you are, the more revelatory, the more chances there are that someone will say, "Oh, I get this. Oh, I wonder what this is about! Why am I responding to this?" Not because I as the author set out to improve you, but because I set out to be honest about myself.

Of course, I didn't come into that clarity easily. I grew up a card-carrying, practicing Catholic in the 1950s and '60s. I remain a practicing Catholic, although you have to practice pretty hard in order to make it work. And so the recognition of being gay—which came upon me in slow stages between the ages of about 15 and 25—meant that I had to uncover myself and discover the depths of my own passion—and by passion I mean love for people, but also passion for the world and passion to live a genuine life, an authentic life that wasn't cribbed and cut to somebody else's pattern.

Understanding that in myself allowed me to put it into the characters that I was writing about, but even more so, it allowed me to assume that people I meet—whom I might not understand—are struggling with the same sort of desire: to connect with their own passion and to be authentic.

It also slowed down my instinct to be judgmental. If you can recognize your own weakness and timidity—"I'm nobody. Who are you? Nobody, too?"—you begin to see: There's a somebody underneath that nobody. And if I can realize how long it took me to find the somebody behind my nobody, then I have the courage and the commitment to be slow and wait—and to trust that there is somebody behind someone else's nobody I might otherwise have dismissed.

That's part of the reason I write the characters I do. The passion that a writer tries to graft into the lives of their characters must in many ways have something to do with the character they recognize in themselves—whether it be a strength that they think they have or maybe a deficit they wish they could fill.

I often laugh and say that Elphaba—my best-known character, based on L. Frank Baum's Wicked Witch of the West—is a lot stronger, smarter, and braver than I ever was. So the passion that I put into creating her was partly a passion of appetite, a passion of need, a passion of wish fulfillment for myself. Sometimes, when I don't know quite how to proceed, I think: What would Elphaba do in this moment?

Now, there are ways I'm not Elphaba. For instance, I'm more patient than she is—more patient with other people and more patient with myself. And I can't do magic and I can't fly like her. But I do long for forgiveness in my life, and for peace, for serenity, for quiet.

Speaking from the heart can expose us, but that vulnerability is where real courage lives. I have an anecdote from the early 1980s—I had a good college friend I had not come out to yet, and I wanted to, but I was afraid I'd lose his friendship. Well, we were on a trip together and I witnessed him directly mocking an effeminate male, and I was agitated on this person's behalf because he was younger and more defenseless. I said to my friend, "You're hurting him. You're hurting me, too. I'm gay. And whenever you make fun of him—whether you mean to or not—you're making fun of me."

I was really terrified, and I could not have said that on my own behalf. But I spoke up because there was somebody else who was more vulnerable than I was, and that person needed my strength more than I needed my own strength. That's where I found the courage in myself.

I knew I could have lost a friend, but I decided to accept that as a debt, in order to defend somebody who was weaker than I was. As it turned out, I didn't lose him. He's still one of my best friends, forty-some years later. And so—it was worth the risk.

If my moral fire hadn't been engaged in having to protect someone who was suffering, I might not have spoken up. And if I hadn't spoken up, I might to this day not have learned how to do it. But having done it once—you recognize you've flexed a muscle you didn't know you had. And every time you flex it, it builds in strength and capacity.

For authors, if you are honest and trust in your work—and don't set out to change the world, but instead focus on giving momentary consolation to whoever might pick up the book—that's enough.

Of course, not every story works for every reader. I've realized over time that my book doesn't work for everyone to get the message across. Some get it through the novel. Others will only understand it through the play or the movie. People respond to different angles, different messages, different windows. One size doesn't fit all.

But anybody who uses story as a tool to communicate is very, very happy if they think there is going to be one person in the history of the world whose life might be improved, touched, or refined by having had this brief, distant contact with your own soul and spirit, as expressed in your story. That's all you can hope for. And if you get two people who feel that way—well, that's double the bang for the buck.

On stage and in the film, the true heartbeat of *Wicked* is felt in the Ozdust Ballroom scene, when Elphaba is finally seen and recognized for being valuable. She had arrived at a moment in her life where she no longer believed that she's somebody. She thinks she's nobody. And then—somebody sees her. And she becomes somebody.

And at the heart of it all for me, I want to make things less hard for people in my path. Whether it be my spouse, my children, my siblings, my readers, the people in my neighborhood, the people in my nation, the people on our globe. I want my time to have been worth it. I want not to have cost the world more than I took from it.

That, to me, is impact.

• • •

My First Flicker

That thing that keeps calling to you, tapping on your brain or tugging at your heart? That's the Pull, and in the emerging phase of your impact journey, it is essentially your awakening. It's beginning to heat you up. Consider the voice that's whispering *this matters* to be the first flicker that has the potential to light a fire, if you let it.

So often we can look back on life and identify those flickering micro-moments that are forever etched in our memories, tied to a Pull that stays with us. These micro-moments are important because, in the Firestarter model, they're often the earliest sparks that reveal what matters to us. They may seem small in the moment, but they can become the reference points we return to again and again as our journey unfolds.

Sometimes these micro-moments have an immediate impact, while at other times their deeper meaning becomes clear much later. For Gregory, the moment of reading, and so deeply connecting with the poem at age 13—"I am nobody. Who are you?"—was instantly formative. It sparked the realization that stories are a powerful tool that could speak to people in profound and personal ways. Only later did he come to fully understand how deeply the fairy tales he read as a child had also been shaping his impact journey.

I vividly remember a key "flicker" micro-moment on my own journey. A Pull came on so strong, clearly signaling I needed to do *something* that would allow me to have a more positive impact on the world. I didn't know what that *something* was, but I remember the experience like it was yesterday.

I had been working at a video game company as the executive assistant to the president. It was a great place to work. The environment was creative and low-stress, and I was surrounded by smart, fun people. I was young, with no major responsibilities, and at a point where I was still in career-exploration mode, having no idea what I "wanted to do with my life."

One day, in a classic watercooler moment, I was chatting with two developers who were talking about a new game they were creating. They were completely lit up, passionately describing the heroine and her signature weapon: a long, barbed wire lasso that she could whip at people to tear their bodies apart, limb by limb. They thought it was badass. I thought it was horrific.

It was like something cracked open in me. Their excited energy, where everything felt so vibrant and positive to them, hit me in the exact opposite way. I thought: *What am I doing here? Am I seriously helping put this kind of violence into the world?* Followed by: *I hate violence. I hate gore. I don't even like video games!*

In that instant, a tidal wave hit: *This is not what I'm meant to do on this Earth.* It wasn't judgment, and it wasn't about the people around me. It was an undeniable sense that I was walking the wrong path. It wasn't just the wrong job—I was heading in the wrong direction.

I sensed a spark beginning to flicker inside of me, fueled by anger, frustration, confusion, shame, and a desperate kind of motivation. And in that environment, I realized I was the outlier.

Similar to Gregory, I felt a Pull telling me I needed to find my own way to "make this world a better place" (as cliché as that sounds). I didn't know what that would look like, but I knew it was time for me to course-correct.

I went home that day, sat in my backyard, and started flipping through the UCLA graduate school catalog that I had randomly picked up months earlier. It was a big, thick book filled with every program they offered. I had no idea what I was looking for. But I knew I needed to find a better way forward, and this was where I began exploring.

And then it happened, as if lightning struck. I saw the name of a program that leapt off the page to me. I didn't know exactly what it entailed or where it might lead me. But I knew, without question, that my journey was about to take a turn. After catching my breath, I circled the program with a pen.

Looking back, that moment represents one of the first times I truly tapped into my fire—before I even had language for it. Before I had a framework. But it was there. That first flicker.

Recognizing the Pull

The first step on any impact journey is recognizing that flicker inside. It often means getting quiet enough to hear your own thoughts and feelings, even when they seem uncertain or intimidating. This alone can feel like a Courageous moment—a willingness to let those whispers exist without rushing past them.

Now, after many years of working alongside leaders and aspiring changemakers, I know how often this step gets skipped. People have a tendency to jump straight into action without having a strong understanding of their Pull or motivation—factors that should form the foundation of one's unique approach to making an impact. I am not suggesting to avoid quickly moving toward action, but I am saying that when it comes to longer-term sustainability, it's extremely helpful to understand where that drive inside of you comes from.

And then there are those who never begin the journey. They become paralyzed by fear of potential backlash or conflict. They assume they should "stay in their lane" or believe they don't have the ability to make a difference. Sometimes they're unsure of exactly what to do or say, so they never allow themselves to explore what might be possible.

But those who nurture that quiet, persistent nudge give themselves the chance to keep moving toward the change they long to see in the world.

Often, that flicker is first recognized when you least expect it. And while it might feel small at the time, it can ultimately end up being life changing. Gregory was reading a poem. I was chatting with colleagues at a water cooler. My friend Cynthia Occelli, who inspires me and so many others, felt her first flicker—the Pull that would shape her life's direction—just before her son was born.

A Pull to a New Future—*Cynthia Occelli*

I was 19, pregnant, and sitting in the lobby of the Social Services building applying for welfare. My child's father was in prison, and I'd quit school in the ninth grade. Surrounded by other pregnant girls, many of whom already had several children, I saw my future. I felt I'd earned it. I'd made all the wrong choices. Sure, I was young, but I'd known they were bad choices when I made them.

Thinking of my unborn son's future made me nauseous. Four young Black boys—my first boyfriend, his best friend, and their two brothers—had recently been killed. My Black son would grow up there. He wasn't even born, and I'd already jeopardized his future. He deserved better.

For months I roiled in guilt, regret, and shame. I wished I'd been a better person.

The birth of my son filled me with overwhelming love. Looking at his tiny brown hand wrapped around my finger filled me with fire. I had to reach for a better life. We had to get out.

That moment changed everything.

I vowed we would have a better life, or I'd spend the rest of my life trying to create one. There was no turning back. I took comfort in the realization that when you're at the bottom, there's only one direction to go. Up.

What followed was an all-encompassing transformation. I worked hard to improve myself by surrendering victimhood, cultivating discipline, avoiding negative habits, becoming independent of others' opinions, and learning to like and respect myself. I walked away from every single person tethered to the life I left. I shattered all the limiting belief patterns I discovered and disciplined myself to believe I can create seemingly impossible outcomes.

I listened to that voice inside of me, and it led me to a life where now I dedicate my days to empowering women, helping them discover and nurture the incredible life force, talents, gifts, and capabilities residing within, leading them to live their highest potential. Overcoming significant personal challenges and reaching incredible milestones has been key to my success in this endeavor. The journey itself forged my capabilities. I was destined for this work. My life path prepared me for it.

• • •

Why the First Flicker Matters

Cynthia's belief in her ability to create seemingly impossible outcomes began with the Pull she felt in the Social Services lobby—an unshakable drive to create a better future for herself and her son. That drive carried her through graduating in the top 3 percent of her law school class, becoming an accomplished author, radio host, and speaker, serving on nonprofit boards, and—most proudly—raising two remarkable children. She recently added "proud grandmother" to that list. Today, the change reAction that ignited in that lobby continues to ripple outward as she coaches high-achieving women to turn major life challenges into transformations and channel those gains into creating positive change in the world.

Be it in the quiet of holding a newborn or in the lines of a poem, that first flicker often arrives as a whisper long before it has the strength to become a roar. For some, it's a lingering voice that keeps asking the same question or delivering a clear, undeniable message. For others, it's a thought or feeling that returns again and again, even if its meaning isn't yet clear. However it shows up, that's the Pull—and it's asking you to pay attention, because whatever this bigger thing is, it matters to you deeply.

I've supported many people who seemed to be waiting for complete clarity before acting on their Pull. In my experience, clarity rarely comes from thinking alone—you often need to take some form of action before it reveals itself.

Recognizing that early signal and choosing to respond, even in small ways, is what allows real progress to begin. At times, that first Pull asks us to turn inward—changing something within ourselves before we can take a stand for others, as it did for Cynthia and me. Other times it can be ignited by the needs or struggles of someone else. Gregory described it beautifully: "I spoke up because there was somebody else who was more vulnerable than I was, and that person needed my strength . . . That's where I found the courage in myself."

Gregory, Cynthia, and I each chose to pay attention to our flickers. Doing so not only moved us toward meaningful impact, but also deepened our sense of purpose—and changed the trajectory of our lives.

The "first flicker" isn't a one-time event. It can appear at many points in life and in connection to different things. New flickers often emerge as we evolve, gain new experiences, and respond to a changing world. For Firestarters, this means our impact journey, sense of purpose, and life trajectory can keep shifting as new

Pulls arise. Even over the last year, I felt a fresh flicker come on strong—one that led to another macro-movement in my impact journey. You'll hear how that unfolds later, but it's a reminder that new flickers can emerge at any stage, even when your path feels set.

When something keeps stirring inside you and won't go away, give yourself permission to trust that it matters and start tuning in to it.

For some, this whole "listen and understand it" idea might feel oversimplified—or even frustrating. You may be filled with emotion, sensing you should be doing something to create change in yourself or the world, but not knowing what that is or where to begin. I can't give you your answers, but I can offer three simple ways to help you tune in and actively work toward understanding what that Pull might be trying to tell you. Each approach offers a different way to tune in—whether you prefer to write, talk, or listen to yourself. I recommend capturing your insights in a dedicated Impact Journal.

When something keeps stirring inside you and won't go away, give yourself permission to trust that it matters and start tuning in to it.

EXERCISE: TUNING INTO YOUR PULL

Write to Yourself

Actively notice and capture patterns and connections any time you feel the Pull. Create a written record of what's going on in your:

- Mind (thoughts, memories, visions)
- Heart (feelings, emotions)
- Body (where it shows up in your body, and what physical sensations are present in that moment)

Every so often, review past entries and note any new clarity or insights about the Pull.

Talk to Yourself

Use self-interview questions to notice and explore what the Pull might be telling you. Treat it like a conversation, not an interrogation. Ask yourself these questions that build on each other:

1. Can you describe the thought/feeling/experience that keeps Pulling at you over and over?
2. Why does that matter to you?
3. Ask again: Why does *that* matter to you? (Peel back another layer.)
4. And again: Why does *that* matter to you? (Peel back even further.)

Come back to these questions from time to time, especially if you find yourself stuck or circling the same thought or feeling. Repeating the exercise can help you notice shifts in your answers and deepen your understanding of what the Pull is asking of you.

Listen to Yourself

Find a quiet place with no distractions and set a timer for 10 minutes. Close your eyes and take deep, steady breaths. When you feel ready, focus on a thought, image, word, or phrase that keeps Pulling at you. Welcome it, give it space, and notice what it stirs in you. Repeat it to yourself if it helps you stay connected. If something feels overwhelming, acknowledge it, set it aside, and gently return your focus to your chosen thought, image, or phrase.

After 10 minutes, note any clarity or insights about the Pull.

Give It Time

I'll be the first to admit: It isn't always easy to understand what your Pull is trying to tell you. Hang in there. Sometimes life needs to unfold a bit more before clarity reveals itself.

What will help—without question—is getting clear on what truly matters to you. Your values, and the Passion that lives in your heart, become the fuel that powers change. We'll explore this more in the chapters ahead.

Whether it begins in our own transformation or in response to another's need, the Pull is a signal. It's asking us to step forward—sometimes for ourselves, sometimes for others—and to trust that even the smallest step can lead to meaningful change.

Here's what I can say after decades of doing this work: If you honor that flicker, reflect on it, and try to understand what it's asking of you, you're already further along your impact journey than most people ever get. I've seen it happen in coaching conversations, in workshops, and even in quiet moments with friends—it's often the smallest recognition that sparks the biggest steps.

So the invitation, while not always easy, is simple: Slow down enough to acknowledge the Pull, begin to understand what it's telling you, and be willing to take even the smallest next step forward.

REFLECTING ON EMERGING PULL

- What's been tugging at you lately? Describe a past micro-moment or recent thought, feeling, or idea that keeps resurfacing—and why it might matter.
- If you're feeling that Pull right now, is it calling you to change something within yourself, or to respond to the needs of others?
- What's one small way you could give this Pull more space in your life, even if you're not ready to act on it yet?
- If this Pull led to something better, what would "better" look like—for you, for others, or for the world around you?
- What might make it easier to keep paying attention to this Pull, so it doesn't fade into the background?

Want to see a clip from Tom's conversation with Gregory Maguire?

Scan the QR Code below or visit www.thenextlevelimpact.com/firestarter-videos

The Heat Means You're Close

If you can't stand the heat, get out of the kitchen.
—Harry S. Truman

Now I know I have a heart, because it's breaking.
—Tin Man, *The Wizard of Oz* (1939)

The Journey So Far

Even if you're not sure exactly where this impact journey is taking you, there's one thing you do know: It's meant to lead to positive change. You've chosen to walk this path because you're a good person with a good heart. You're not the kind of traveler who leaves a trail of trash behind—you're the one picking up the mess others have left along the way.

When it's unclear which way to go, you take out a map. You see right away this hasn't been a straight path—it's been full of twists and turns, with countless intersecting trails behind you. Some you chose with intention and others were completely random. As you trace that windy path with your finger you see how you arrived at this exact spot. Looking ahead, you see so many more paths to choose from, each taking you in an unknown direction.

You know it's time to move forward, especially because this path is starting to grow colder and darker. As you decide which way to turn, you notice one of the paths in front of you feels warmer than the others. You take a few steps toward it and feel its warmth inviting you to come closer. That's when you realize how you'll choose your direction from now on: Follow the heat.

I Felt the Heat Rise

I circled the UCLA graduate program with a pen for a second time: *Master of Education: Counseling in Student Affairs.* It was as though a new path had just presented itself before me, and as I began imagining myself walking toward it, I was already beginning to feel some internal sparks generating heat.

Why was this energy suddenly building inside me? My mind was rapidly beginning the process of **connecting the dots**—the smaller but significant micro-moments, the larger and more life-shifting macro-movements, and the values taking shape in me. They were all converging in a way that was starting to make sense. I'm not sure I could have arrived at this moment any other way, had it not been for those sparks throughout my life and the discovery of this program that would ultimately change my trajectory.

Connect the dots, connect the dots, connect the dots . . .

Big bold dot #1: UCLA. This was a place I had dreamed about attending ever since I was a child. Granted, this might have been because I had envisioned morning classes by the sea, classrooms converted into beach-volleyball courts for afternoon students-vs-instructors matches, and days ending singing Kumbaya as the sun set over the ocean. Not exactly reality, but young Tommy sure did have a colorful imagination!

Big surprise dot #2: Student Affairs. I had never before considered it as a career path—and for good reason. The profession is grounded in Higher Education, and I did *not* have a great college experience. That listing immediately took my mind away from my beautiful SoCal backyard and over to the biting winter air of my undergraduate campus in Massachusetts. The contrast was staggering. Real time: feeling safe and free, with the warm sun on my skin and my partner nearby. Flashback: one of the hardest periods of my life—a time filled with fear, loneliness, and feeling trapped in the closet that kept me from being my authentic self.

I never wanted to live through that type of suffocating experience again, but I didn't want others to have to experience it either. The words "Student Affairs" kept running through my mind. I began thinking back to my work-study job in the Class Deans' Office, a function of Student Affairs at my undergrad. I thought about how those deans treated me with care and respect. One dean in particular, Carol Hacker, was phenomenal—to this day she *still* makes a point of checking in on me. I never let on to her, or really anyone, how much I was struggling in college, but she, along with other Student Affairs practitioners, were genuinely invested in my well-being. They modeled something powerful, and in that reflective moment I realized: *I want to be that kind of person for others.*

Later that year, I applied, was accepted, and enrolled in the UCLA program. At orientation, I learned that I had to choose an assistantship where I would work in one of the many Student Affairs offices on campus. I remember walking around the UCLA campus, feeling a little less spark as I considered more familiar options like the Career Center or Residential Life. Then I saw it: a painted sidewalk sign standing outside of a campus building, welcoming me into a whole new world.

Big rainbow dot #3: The LGBT Campus Resource Center. In that instant, my inner heat surged—Passion rushing in like oxygen to a flame. I had never heard of a college LGBTQ+ center. I walked inside and found the most welcoming space, led by one of the kindest, most inspiring people I'd ever met: Dr. Ronni Sanlo.

Little did I realize that Ronni was not only a recognized pioneer in college LGBTQ+ centers, but she had literally *written the books* on the topic. I introduced myself, and within moments it was clear to me how special she and this space were. Apparently, she saw something in me during that first interaction as well. As I was leaving, she presented me with the final critical dot.

Big vocational dot #4: "You should do your assistantship here." My journey—and the Passion driving it—had led me back to a college campus, a place I once swore I'd never return to. An environment where caterpillars are meant to turn into butterflies, yet in my earlier experience, I didn't have the opportunity to do so. I suddenly felt such a strong sense of purpose: I needed to help others experience their own metamorphosis by creating an environment that supported that process rather than hindered it.

And by **connecting these dots**, I began to experience a metamorphosis of my own. That year changed my life forever.

Following Your Heat

While Pull is shaped by the moments we've lived through and the identities we carry, Passion is what means the most to us—what's calling the loudest. When you feel yourself heating up inside, that's a Passion signal, pointing to the fuel for your inner fire. It may be the most essential of the three elements in the Firestarter Model, because without Passion you're unlikely to take meaningful action.

Even for natural-born Firestarters, there's no single way to identify the source of heat that's going to light you up. When your emotions heighten—whether sparked by joy, anger, creativity, or truth—it's your heart's way of saying *this matters*. Passion doesn't always roar; sometimes it's a quiet whisper . . . the sacred, insistent kind that draws you in and keeps you moving forward.

For me, that heat initially began to rise due to strong feelings of discontent in my work. I didn't jump right into "just get a new job" mode. I instead started thinking about my values and what mattered most to me and reflecting on significant micro-moments and macro-movements. Today, when I'm coaching clients who are on their own discovery journeys, I follow a similar process: having them first reflect on their values and the moments that have shaped them—connecting the big dots before jumping into "what's next."

That process led me to a new discovery (and career): I cared deeply about supporting others through inclusion and empowerment. My mind had to connect those dots over a long stretch of time before I could see where my Passions converged—and where the heat was most intense.

Over time, I've recognized that our own Passion often draws us toward people who have a similar fire in them. It's as though once you know the feel of your own heat, you recognize it in others. It radiates from them and draws you in. One person in whom I sensed it so strongly is my dear friend Sherri Shepherd, who came into my life 25 years ago—maybe by luck, but more likely by fate. From the start, the alignment was undeniable, and there was no way I was letting go of this incredible Firestarter.

Sherri is fueled to put more positivity into the world through joy . . . the kind that makes people feel lighter, seen, and connected. Now let me be real: As big as our smiles can be, neither of us is walking around laughing and grinning ear-to-ear all the time. We've experienced and carried each other through plenty of life's hardships, and we share a deep empathy (and frustration) about the struggles and rapidly increasing divisiveness we see in the world. But one of the reasons we're so connected is that instead of letting those trials drag us down, they push us to find ways to lift people up.

Sherri's Passion for drawing smiles and laughter—on her talk show, on the comedy stage, and in the characters she plays—isn't just entertainment. It's about bypassing politics, prejudice, and pain to remind us of our shared humanity. She knows that when joy and connection flow together, people soften, open up, and begin to see each other differently. That's the fire she always carries with her, and the throughline I've seen play out in every role she takes on in life.

Fueled to Uplift—*Sherri Shepherd*

There's that saying: "You've got more good years behind you than ahead of you." And as hard as that is to hear, it lit a fire in me. It made me start thinking seriously about my mortality—about what I want to pass down and how I want to use my voice while I still have it.

Because life has kicked me in my ass. And then helped me up. And then slapped the mess out of me again. And I kept getting up. That's the story. That's the power. Not just the laughter or the lights or the roles, but the fact that I've kept showing up. And showing up with heart.

I think I always knew I had a great story—something entertaining, something funny. But I didn't fully realize how much that story could actually help people until recently. Probably within the last few years,

I started asking: "What legacy do I want to leave behind? What do I want people to think about me when I'm gone?"

That's when I realized: I'm not just here to entertain. I've got life wisdom. I've got gems. And the things life has put me through—the hard stuff, the painful stuff, the moments I wasn't sure I'd survive—they've all taught me I have something worth sharing.

Especially for women in their fifties—women who don't feel seen. They're like, "I can't get a man. I can't get a job. Nobody's paying attention to me anymore." But then they see me, and they go, "Wait a minute—she's still here. She's still laughing. She's still doing the damn thing." And they want to hear that story.

Even when it comes to my health—people used to think I just wanted to fit into some jeans. No. I'm trying to live. I'm trying to stay alive for my son Jeffrey. And I feel an urgency with that. Because he needs me. And I want to be here.

But it's more than that. The world needs more kindness. More humanity. And it scares me where we're at right now—how quick people are to turn it off, to stop seeing each other. When I think about leaving Jeffrey behind in a world like this it terrifies me. That's why I lead with joy.

Because here's what I know: Laughter doesn't have a color. It doesn't have a culture. It just is. It comes from the soul. And when people laugh—really laugh—it connects us. It softens us. And it heals us.

That's the fire in me. That's my protest. That's my power. To bring joy when the world feels hard. To be a resting place for people when they're exhausted from the headlines and the hurt. That's what I'm building.

And sometimes, staying in the fire means staying in the discomfort. Like when I was filming the movie *Straw*. Taraji P. Henson was in it—crying hysterically, just killing this scene. And I'm in the back like, "Okay God, I'm supposed to be crying, too. Please let me cry!" Nothing. I tried every trick in the book. I whispered to myself, "Cry, bitch, cry!" Still nothing.

And I spiraled. I thought I was gonna look weak. I thought I had failed. But when I saw the final cut, it clicked. I wasn't supposed to cry. My character was the anchor, the grounding force. The one who held it together. And if I had cried, it wouldn't have hit the same.

God dried up my tears for a reason. That experience taught me to trust myself—even in the moment of panic. Even when everything in you says, "You're not doing it right." That feeling of self-doubt? Sometimes it's a sign you're actually aligned.

When things get hard, I've learned to pause and ask: "Am I close to something meaningful?"

I've felt that again and again, especially with my talk show. So many people have told me to stay in my lane and don't rock the boat. But I know what I want to do and who I want to bring to the table.

Flame Monroe is one of my dearest friends. She's transgender, brilliant, funny as hell. And for years, I fought to get her on talk shows, and kept getting told no. But when I got my own show? I said, "Damn it, she's gonna be on it." It wasn't easy. I had to push. But she came on. And she killed.

Same with the queens from *RuPaul's Drag Race*. I brought them on not just for the sparkle, but because I knew someone watching would feel seen. That's how change happens—one laugh, one moment, one person at a time.

Sometimes, when the front door's locked, you gotta find a side door. Or kick it down altogether.

That's how the podcast *Two Funny Mamas* was born. I had been pitching talk shows, getting told no over and over. It was devastating. But my girlfriend said, "Why do you keep asking for permission? Give yourself permission." Then we walked to her driveway, and right on top of a "free books" pile was a book I had written—*Permission Slips.* That felt like a sign.

We couldn't even record the podcast in a studio because of the pandemic. So we did it from home. And people listened. A man from Korea reached out and said he laughed so hard he crashed his bike. A woman told us her mother with Alzheimer's still lights up when she hears our voices. We raised money for teachers and sent headphones to an entire school for kids with special needs. That podcast has changed lives. And it changed mine.

That's the thing about impact: Sometimes it comes from the places you'd least expect it. Being Jeffrey's mother has had the greatest impact on me. He's on the spectrum. He's smart, funny, sensitive, and he trusts me. And through him, I've learned compassion—not the performative kind, but deep, soul-level compassion that reshapes how you walk through the world.

I think my greatest impact is being a mother. Sometimes I don't feel like it is, but I can see it—especially with Jeffrey, and how he's navigating the world.

And honestly, it changed me. Being his mom, and learning to accept him as he is, opened something in me.

Like that time I was going through my divorce. I was tired. I was broken. And that's when you, Tom, and your husband Jimmy—my two dear friends—invited me to visit. You two told me, "Go sleep. We've got Jeffrey." And you meant it. You just loved him.

You didn't care that he was a little Black boy. You didn't care what he said—some of the stuff that came out of his mouth! You just loved on him. No judgment. No conditions. Just kindness. Just love.

That stayed with me. Because in the very religious world I came from, love often came with conditions. Compassion came with rules. But here were two gay men loving my child so fully and so freely that it planted something deep in me and there was a shift.

What I learned from that weekend with you both is that compassion can go a long way. And it doesn't have to be loud, it just has to be real.

Now I'm big on compassion. I believe in stepping across the threshold and getting to know someone you never thought you would. Maybe it's a Muslim woman. Maybe it's someone you were taught to judge. But when you look past all that and just see the person who wants their kids to be safe, to play, to laugh, to grow—that's when you get to the heart of it.

And compassion? That's what makes us human.

• • •

Passion with a Purpose

Sherri's story reminds us that one person's fire—when fueled by Passion—can spark a change reAction, creating ripples of joy, healing, and connection far beyond what they may ever see.

Sometimes the fuel for your fire comes from your own lived experience—the calling you couldn't possibly ignore or the moments that upended life as you knew it and demanded a response. And sometimes it comes from someone else's need, tugging at your heart with such force that you know you *have* to act. Either way, Passion is born from connection—to our own story or the stories of others.

Yvonne Mann's story is a little of both. Her love for Maui and music started as a way to bring people together, to create something joyful in her community. Over time, she began to see how music could also heal, how it could respond to hardship in ways words alone couldn't. And then, when wildfires devastated the island, her Passion found a new purpose: helping her community recover, one song, one gathering, one moment of hope at a time.

Fueled to Heal—*Yvonne Mann*

If we listen to our inner voice, our purpose is right in front of us. I wasn't sitting around trying to design an "impact plan." Without a doubt, I am doing something that makes no logical sense—it was because of being open to new connections, leaning into them, NOT being fearful to ask questions, and having faith to jump off the cliff.

There was no specific inspiration . . . it was a moment while on Maui when I felt there needed to be a music experience for the people and visitors to Maui. I wrote the idea down on a napkin while having fish tacos at Tommy Bahama in Wailea. The event happened and grew from that. The Maui Songwriters Festival has now been going strong for over a decade, and we are creating similar events in other locations across the US. Tommy Bahama, home to where that first spark happened, has been one of our main sponsors the entire time.

I have always felt music is medicine and is most definitely healing. A song can flood your mind with memories, happy to sad. That belief became even more real for me after the 2023 Lahaina wildfires. During our 10-year anniversary, the Maui Songwriters Festival put on an assembly at one of the schools in Lahaina that was in a temporary location because their school was destroyed during the fires. The Air Force Band of the Pacific, from Pearl Harbor, and three singer-songwriters came and performed for these children and their families who had lost so much. The music brought them joy—and they gave that joy back to us tenfold.

The resilience of Maui locals is phenomenal. I attribute it to the community supporting itself, friends, families, and religious communities in particular and their very spiritual and *Ohana* nature. They are very gracious and grateful for all the support they get from everyday people.

I receive a generous amount of appreciation in return acknowledging the difference this event makes to the community. I also have the joy of seeing new relationships bloom and new collaborations created between locals, artists, and songwriters. I do what I do because I love it and have the honor to observe the difference music makes in people's lives . . . songwriters write the soundtracks of our lives.

The artists and songwriters have worked extremely hard to get where they are—they understand life's struggles (their songs play that out) and they are so giving. This year I watched our songwriters spend private time/days with the locals at their homes and see the island from the locals' perspective. Our artists gave back generously and encouraged festival attendees to do the same. In the past three years, because of this generosity the Maui Songwriters Festival has given $220,000 to the community of Maui.

We all really DO know what we need to do. We just don't want to listen sometimes because it might be hard and there might be a failure. But failure is not failure unless you quit. So listen to your heart (GOD), your gut (intuition / Holy Spirit) and your positive thoughts. If they all align—and they will when it is right—follow it. Jump off the cliff with faith and let go of the fear—you truly "got this."

• • •

The Heat That Guides You: Connecting Your ~~Dots~~ Stars

Your Passion might already have you fired up, and where you're heading (or needing to head) might be clear as day to you. If so, amazing.

But if you're still feeling unsure about your own source of fuel, I encourage you to take the pressure off yourself—your Passion doesn't have to reveal itself all at once. For some, that clarity comes in a single moment; for others, it unfolds slowly over time, shaped by sparks that appear when you least expect them. You can't always force that kind of discovery, but you *can* create space to understand it more clearly.

If you feel stuck—like you're looking outward, feet planted on the ground, but unsure which path to take next—try looking up to the stars for help.

EXERCISE: CONNECTING YOUR STARS

For centuries, travelers have used the night sky to find their way. Close your eyes (or step outside under a clear sky) and imagine each star as something that matters to you: a person, an experience, a cause, a value, maybe even a Passion or purpose. Notice which ones shine brightest right now, and how they seem to relate to each other. Spend some time stargazing—the vast sky above holds infinite space and possibility.

Now grab your Impact Journal and write:

- What do the brightest stars represent to you?
- If any of those bright stars were connected, would a new image appear—something you hadn't noticed before?
- What else came up for you?

Maybe, like Sherri, you connected hardship with creating joy through shared human experiences. Maybe, like me, you connected part of your identity with a specific life experience and a calling you hadn't considered before. Maybe, like Yvonne, you connected one of your interests with your community and an unexpected need.

When the stars in your life connect, their constellation becomes more than a picture—it becomes your guide. Whether that guide presents itself to you now or at some point in the future, trust that it's already written somewhere in the stars . . . you might just need to give it time before you can see it more clearly.

If you feel like you could use more support, remember this: Stargazing doesn't have to be done alone. I've learned from my own impact journey and from coaching other changemakers that hard-to-spot constellations are often easier to chart with help from fellow Firestarters.

REFLECTING ON EMERGING PASSION

- Which "stars" from your life story are currently grabbing your attention the most, and why?
- What colors do significant micro-moments add to your sky, and why?
- What values feel like your North Star—most central to who you are and how you live?
- Where does the sky light up most when you imagine having a meaningful impact?
- What role do (or could) fellow Firestarters in your orbit play in adding fuel to your fire?

Want to see a clip from Tom's conversation with Sherri Shepherd?

Scan the QR Code below or visit www.thenextlevelimpact.com/firestarter-videos

Strike the Match

I am no longer accepting the things I cannot change.
I am changing the things I cannot accept.
—Angela Davis

True courage is in facing danger when you are afraid.
—Cowardly Lion, *The Wonderful Wizard of Oz* (1900)

The Ignition Point

Chances are, throughout life you've felt all sorts of Pulls tugging at your heartstrings and tapping at your brain. You're an empathetic person (I assume, since you're reading this book), so those "something should be done" feelings will likely keep surfacing in response to what's happening in and around you.

But then there are those times when the Pull comes on much stronger, demanding your attention. You feel the heat building inside you as Passion kicks in, signaling that something needs to change. It's as if your whole body is insisting *this matters—do something.*

This is where all those micro-moments that once seemed small begin to add up, compounding into a potential macro-movement. Life's journey is about to morph into an impact journey—if you choose to be brave.

The ingredients are there. The question is: Do you have the Courage to strike the match and ignite the fire in you?

> *Do you have the Courage to strike the match and ignite the fire in you?*

You know one thing for sure: Going down this path likely won't make life easier. In fact, it feels almost guaranteed to make it harder. Impact requires action, action requires change, and change is uncomfortable. And this is something you're considering doing intentionally?

So you have a choice to make: Stick with the status quo and *play it safe*, or lean in with Courage and *be the change*.

When your Pull creates the spark, your Passion provides the fuel, and you allow Courage to become your ignition, that's a defining macro-movement in your impact journey.

Why? Because all three elements have aligned.

IT LIT A FIRE.

You not only envision the change ahead, but you are now part of it . . . and it is part of you. You are a Firestarter.

How Courage Catches

The first time I realized Courage could be a force for change was in my own coming-out process.

I was terrified to understand who I was, let alone accept and love myself. That would require accepting that I was (am) gay and eventually coming out. For much of my life, I believed denial—or even death—were safer options than living as my authentic self. I grew up in a time and place without any openly LGBTQ+ people in my life, and I definitely didn't see anyone in the media who was out, celebrated, and thriving. Quite the opposite. Back then, in my world, being gay was almost always associated with the same two words: abomination and AIDS.

Still, as a scared and closeted kid, I remember sensing something in certain men that struck a deep chord in me. Greg Louganis—widely considered the world's greatest springboard diver—who left me in awe every time I watched him compete on TV. George Michael—whose voice and lyrics connected to my soul in ways I could barely comprehend. My kind, funny (and admittedly very cute) hairdresser—who unknowingly gave me a sense of safety and comfort for the 30 minutes I sat in his chair each month, something I felt nowhere else in the world. I couldn't name it then, but I knew I saw pieces of myself in all of them.

I eventually experienced the impactful micro-moments of Greg Louganis publicly coming out while I was in high school, and George Michael doing so when I was in college. Their Courageous pride ignited a change reAction, helping me (and countless others) begin to understand and accept myself. Right after college, I moved 3,000 miles away to Los Angeles and suddenly started meeting openly gay people *in real life*. Talk about experiencing a macro-movement shift.

I felt like I was watching these people risk *everything*, but the reward of freedom actually made it worth it. Finally, I too decided to allow Courage to overcome fear. This was my ignition moment: I chose my own freedom—meaning *truly* living—as an out and proud gay man. I did it for myself, but in a full-circle moment, I also knew others who felt scared or alone might benefit from seeing parts of themselves reflected in me.

If I wanted to live in a world where people could feel accepted, safe, and celebrated simply for being themselves, then I had to be Courageous and own my role in creating that change.

By choosing to be brave and opening my heart to the world, I suddenly felt the presence of countless others like me—past, present, and future—who I had never been aware of before. For the first time, I could celebrate all of us collectively, while also now understanding how indebted I was to those who had paved the path I was finally able to walk.

Whoever you are, whatever your truth, know this: living authentically, owning your uniqueness with pride, and modeling that for others is an incredibly powerful act of Courage. It won't just transform your life; it will also ripple outward, creating a change reAction that transforms the lives of others.

Know this: living authentically, owning your uniqueness with pride, and modeling that for others is an incredibly powerful act of Courage.

• • •

Twenty years after my own coming-out journey, I was shocked to see Greg Louganis tagged in a photo one of my friends posted on social media. I decided to once again be brave and send Greg a message thanking him for the impact he had on me as a young, closeted gay boy. To my surprise, my childhood hero did what I've seen so many changemakers do—he responded, and as fate would have it, we became connected Firestarters.

Greg himself is living proof of a change reAction: When he chose to publicly share his truth about being gay (in 1994) and about living with HIV (in 1995), it didn't just change his own life. His Courage sparked shifts that saved lives, changed perceptions, and lit the way for countless others.

In his own words, here's how Greg found the strength to live bravely in his authenticity, and the impact it's had ever since.

The Courage to Live One's Truth—*Greg Louganis*

I had trained to compartmentalize. I learned that lesson early.

I was in dance and acrobatics before I began diving, and when I was nine or ten I remember smacking my foot on a beam and it was really painful, but I wrapped it up and didn't tell anybody because I didn't want to get pulled from performing. Years later, I slammed my hands together during a practice dive for the 1984 Diving Nationals, and knew I injured something but I dove anyway, because there was a record I had to break. And in the 1988 Olympic Games in Seoul—when I hit my head on the springboard [and went on to win the gold medal]—people asked "How did you do that?" Well, I trained to do that: to compartmentalize. I had practiced those skills, to hit your head on the board, come back and still win—to push through.

Is that healthy? Not particularly, but you can pick it up later to address it. And it doesn't necessarily come with a lot of trauma when it's more of a decision that you make—I'm going to get on the board and try to be as successful as I can be for this moment in time. I'm going to do this anyway.

In the early '90s, I was performing in the play *Jeffrey* in New York. I was playing a character named Darius—an out, proud gay man who was open about his HIV status. At the time, my own HIV status was still a secret. So I was on stage, night after night, facing my fears while celebrating that character's honesty.

This was still a time when you didn't talk about that stuff. You'd be a liability if you came forward with your HIV status. More education was happening, but there was still a lot of stigma surrounding HIV/AIDS. For the most part, the only people who were coming out were going into the hospital and they couldn't deny it.

I felt like I was on an island, with barely a phone for communication to the outside world. But I was confident I wasn't alone. The one thought that kept pulling at me was, "The truth shall set you free."

I didn't want to wait until I was in a hospital bed, like Rock Hudson or Freddie Mercury, before speaking my truth. I wanted to come out—before I was outed—on my own terms. By telling the truth, it would alleviate any concerns about "who am I authentically." I could take my power back.

In Buddhism, it's "What's the next right action?" I just knew that writing my book was the right next step for me.

So I shared my truth—being a gay man, being HIV positive, being bullied, being in an abusive relationship, dyslexia . . . all of these things I had once perceived as weaknesses. After the book came out and I went on tour, I realized something: By sharing my perceived weaknesses, I was actually sharing my strength, because not everybody can do that.

At book signings, thousands of people showed up. Over and over, I heard: "You saved my life." "I came out to my friends and family because of your book." "I told people I'm HIV-positive after reading your story."

It wasn't on my mind that it would have this effect. Because both then and now, I don't know what kind of impact I'm going to have—I have no control over that. So I would have done that anyway—but the impact it had was really incredible; it was a byproduct of doing the right thing.

All I can do is live my life in such a way that I can be proud and be the person who is consistent and walking the walk. There are very few people who walk the walk, but that's who I want to be.

If you're at the beginning of finding your own voice, my advice is simple: listen. Most people just want to hear themselves talk—that's ego. And if you're only listening with your mind, you'll go crazy . . . your mind will lie to you. But if you stay quiet, chances are you'll get your questions answered—your body will tell you the truth, and your heart will tell you the truth.

• • •

Hide It Under a Bushel? No! I'm Gonna Let It Shine

Greg's bravery, in the face of losing everything, remains not just admirable, but historic.

Sometimes it can feel like you're heading in the right direction—internal fire building, self-confidence growing, and a certainty that change is necessary. But then, as your body begins to sense something is about to shift, your mind can take over with questions: Am I doing the right thing? Am I taking the right approach? Am I enough? Am I going to lose something—or maybe even everything?

I think back to the year 2004. At this point, I was trying to live as authentically as possible—open, honest, and proud—which felt scary but also necessary if I wanted to pave the way for others to do the same. On the work front, I was trying my best at the LGBTQ+ center, learning through trial and error and often stumbling my way forward. Supporting students in fragile stages of their lives meant I didn't always get it right. But I came to see that every misstep, though painful, was part of the process, each one marking growth in both consciousness and capability. My heart was in the right place, so I chose to be brave, stayed in the fire, and kept going. (Sidenote: The whole "imperfect and still learning" thing doesn't have an endpoint!)

On the personal front, my partner Jimmy and I knew we were in it for the long haul. Then the news broke: Massachusetts was about to become the first state to legalize same-sex marriage. Not only was this historic, but it was happening in my home state. That quickly led to my teary (okay, maybe a little sappy) proposal—we were ecstatic to solidify our relationship legally and couldn't wait to celebrate with family and friends.

One night, shortly before our engagement announcement was going out, I sat down at my computer and saw a new email from a friend. When I opened it, I was stunned—she had forwarded a petition against same-sex marriage to her contacts. This was someone I adored and couldn't wait to invite to our wedding.

The mental rollercoaster I went through is hard to describe.

- **Emotions:** sadness, anger, confusion, hurt, fear, loss.
- **Questions:** Who could I trust? What did people really think of me—or of Jimmy and me as a couple? Was this

> completely driven by faith? I was raised Christian my whole life . . . am I now a bad Christian? Am I even allowed to still call myself a Christian? Is my loving, committed relationship a bad thing? And if I was this scared, was I even qualified to support other LGBTQ+ people?

I could have deleted the email and kept my head down. Staying silent felt safer. But how could I be a changemaker if I said nothing? A voice inside told me that at a time like this, it was even *more* important to stay open, honest, and proud. On the other hand, how could I reasonably expect to gain acceptance if my "speaking up" came across as a counter-attack? I realized I had to be brave and stand up for what I knew was right—including my own self-acceptance—but do it in a way that wouldn't shut everything down.

I channeled my inner Greg Louganis—who had modeled such an effective mix of soft kindness and brave Courage—and drafted my reply: "Got your email. It really stung. Jimmy and I are in the midst of planning our wedding. If you ever want to hear the other side of this debate, I'd be glad to share with you."

Then I struck the match and hit send.

And instead of her hitting delete, she replied with an apology for not being more considerate, and explained that as a woman of strong faith, we might see things differently.

> *Rather than "calling someone out," try "bringing them in." . . . It takes Courage and vulnerability, but it can be incredibly effective.*

This was one of the first times I tested what has become a go-to strategy for me as a changemaker: Rather than "calling someone out," try "bringing them in." And one of the best ways to do that is by sharing your story. It takes Courage and vulnerability, but it can be incredibly effective.

The doors swung wide open for an honest, unfiltered conversation about the real struggle some people of faith face when reconciling what they've been taught with what they feel in their hearts.

Having grown up in a very religious home myself, I knew this paradox far too well. It was the exact thing that kept me in the self-hating closet for years, hopelessly trying to pray the gay away—desperate to earn God's approval and avoid "eternal damnation in the fires of hell." That struggle was so exhausting and painful that I eventually realized if I didn't choose to love and accept myself for who I was—who God made me—then my own self-hatred would kill me.

During my journey toward self-acceptance, I had read something that proved to be a very important reminder many times later in life: Queer people (like me) should remember how long it took to let go of our own internalized phobias to embrace ourselves—and then, in fairness, be willing to give others *at least* that much time to come around in their own journey of acceptance.

My friend didn't come to the wedding, but our friendship continued. I chose to put any disappointment aside, along with the fear of being judged as sinful, and just live as my proud, authentic self. What carried our friendship forward was our shared values and connection to everyday life, with the paradoxical issue remaining mostly in the background.

I stayed grounded, trusting in myself and in the beautiful family Jimmy and I were building, which soon enough included our two adopted children. My comfort level and confidence in my impact-focused work was also increasing, as my career eventually began to expand beyond serving the LGBTQ+ community alone.

My friend also stayed grounded as her own authentic self—a woman of strong faith who also happened to be one of the most loving, thoughtful, and funny people I've ever known.

And then one morning, I was watching her sitting around a table with her co-workers: Whoopi Goldberg, Joy Behar, Elizabeth Hasselbeck, and Barbara Walters. These women—and my dear friend Sherri—began discussing an LGBTQ+ news story as that day's episode of *The View* was airing on live television.

Suddenly, Sherri began to talk about the love she's witnessed between Jimmy and me, and the love we have for our two children (who refer to her as Auntie Sherri), as well as for her and her son Jeffrey. She then said that if anything ever "happened" to her, she would want us to be the ones to raise her son.

From left: Jimmy and Tom with their children Lukas and Maya; Sherri Shepherd and her son Jeffrey.

My jaw dropped. Just by me being myself—standing in my truth, and doing it with love instead of anger—millions of people around the world were hearing her bravely share an incredibly powerful message of love and acceptance.

Ever since, my dearest friend has not shied away from the conversation of faith reconciliation and LGBTQ+ acceptance—but she addresses it as a fierce ally and advocate, through the lens of love, compassion, and equity. I'm in awe as I watch her consistently push to ensure diverse voices and stories, including those of queer and trans people, are represented on the daytime talk show she now hosts, which carries her name alone.

Courage can be hard to muster when you're early in your Firestarter journey, but it's essential. So when things get tricky, scary, or frustrating—hang in there. When the flame shifts from fire in your belly to fury in your brain—take a deep breath. When you aren't sure if you're making a difference—know that you are.

Strike the match, trust yourself, and trust the universe. You are having an impact, whether you see it or not.

Strike the match, trust yourself, and trust the universe. You are having an impact, whether you see it or not. Maybe it's on one person, or maybe it ignited a change reAction that touches millions. You just never know.

The Many Faces of Courage

Courage can show up in different forms. For Greg, it looked like bold visibility—refusing to stay silent and stepping directly into the fire at the risk of losing everything. For Sherri and me, it required us staying open and grounded, setting aside judgement and discomfort and instead leaning into love, patience, and acceptance.

For my friend and organizational psychologist Dr. Enin Rudel, it was the call to confront systems of injustice head-on, while also building bridges—and then modeling for others how to do the same.

Choosing Courage over Comfort— *Dr. Enin Rudel*

As a Black male, my lived experiences shape how I understand systems, power, and resilience.

I recall an experience in graduate school when it came time to pursue an internship. I was eager to gain clinical experience, specifically within a hospital setting. I met with my field placement advisor at a coffee shop. After 40 minutes of thoughtful conversation, he paused and told me he did not feel comfortable recommending me for a hospital placement.

I remember being stunned. When I asked why, he was unable to offer a clear reason. Weeks later, another professor shared that she had seen a pattern: Hospital placements were often reserved for white students, while students of color were quietly discouraged from "top-tier" opportunities.

That was the moment I realized silence would only reinforce the status quo. Rather than walk away, I became even more determined to pursue a hospital placement despite the barriers. Through persistent networking and outreach, I eventually secured an internship and later, a full-time position as the hospital's first Black male clinician in that department.

That experience taught me something foundational: Systems often don't change on their own. They must be challenged. And sometimes, simply insisting on your right to be there is itself a powerful act of resistance.

At a certain point, I realized I couldn't unsee what I had seen, nor could I unhear what I had heard. Something in me shifted. My perspective deepened, and I began to understand the role I might play in improving the conditions around me. A question kept surfacing, one that I couldn't ignore: "Am I playing my part, or am I simply playing along?"

With that question came a growing sense of responsibility. I came to understand that silence, doing nothing, saying nothing, was a luxury I could not afford.

This was the catalyst for my decision to once again return to school and pursue a doctorate in Organizational Leadership Psychology. That journey gave me the platform to do much of what I'm doing now. Through consulting, coaching, and teaching, I aim to deliver a message rooted in bridge-building and the pursuit of shared understanding.

I began my research on Black male leadership and emotional intelligence just a few months before the murder of George Floyd. His death marked a deeply painful and pivotal moment in our nation's history, one that shook many of us to our core.

A colleague cautioned me that pursuing publishing opportunities on my research topic might carry personal and professional risks, not just for me, but potentially for my family as well. That conversation stayed with me.

But I made a conscious choice to choose courage over comfort and stay the course, even when the road ahead felt uncertain. Because the story I was telling needed (and still needs) to be told.

I have a deep-rooted commitment to creating spaces where people feel heard, seen, valued, and empowered. What has shifted within me is a profound sense of clarity and purpose. I am guided by a clear, unwavering vision of what we could be, and I am determined to play my part in helping us get there. That commitment has only intensified—I've doubled down on this work, unapologetically—because remembering my "why" keeps me grounded in the truth that this is bigger than me, and the stakes have never been higher.

I am deeply purpose-driven. I've always aspired to create spaces where people can show up fully, where their authentic selves are not only welcomed but truly honored. This fire is sustained through meaningful dialogue and deep listening, and it connects to something greater: a belief that healing, justice, and belonging are not distant ideals, but real possibilities, built conversation by conversation, system by system.

For me, the value of emotional intelligence, the power of listening, and the importance of awareness have been integral in shaping my own Firestarter journey, and can be key to others navigating theirs.

• • •

Stepping into the Heat

Courage is so often the sticking point. The Pull can be unrelenting and the Passion tells us we care desperately, but then our mind floods us with all the reasons we should *not* speak up or act:

- It's too risky.
- I don't know what to do or say.
- It's not my place.
- I can't really have an impact.
- It might make things worse.
- I should let someone else deal with it.

That's when you need to tell your mind to STFU. (Silence Those False Underminers!)

Discomfort is something most people are taught to avoid, but for the Firestarter, discomfort is where we lean in and the change begins. This *is* the time to speak up and act, so we need to tell our minds:

- ~~It's too risky.~~ The potential for change is greater than the risk.
- ~~I don't know what to do or say.~~ It might not come out perfect, but silence is not an option.
- ~~It's not my place.~~ The more who step in, the stronger the collective power.
- ~~I can't really have an impact.~~ Even small actions can have an impact.
- ~~It might make things worse.~~ Inaction allows things to get worse.
- ~~I should let someone else deal with it.~~ If I truly care, then I must act.

Here's the hard truth: Sometimes the fire gets uncomfortably hot—not because you're off track, but because you've stepped directly onto the path that leads to impact that truly matters.

Let your spark (Pull), fuel (Passion), and ignition (Courage) come together, and let's see you set this world ablaze, Firestarter.

That heat you're feeling isn't coming from a fire meant to destroy you. It's the kind of fire that is meant to burn away what's no longer needed. And as Mother Nature has taught us, once a fire passes, the soil is so much richer, making way for beautiful new growth to emerge.

So you want to have an impact that truly matters? Then let your spark (Pull), fuel (Passion), and ignition (Courage) come together, and let's see you set this world ablaze, Firestarter.

REFLECTING ON EMERGING COURAGE

- Whose bravery is inspiring and helps you see new possibilities?
- What discomfort in your life might be a signal of meaningful change ahead?
- When have you chosen Courage over comfort and been grateful you did?
- Where do you sense fear holding you back, and what small act of Courage could move you forward?
- What's burning hottest for you right now, asking for your Courage?

Want to see a clip from Tom's conversation with Greg Louganis?

Scan the QR Code below or visit www.thenextlevelimpact.com/firestarter-videos

PART TWO

ONGOING

Build While It Burns

Faith is taking the first step,
even when you don't see the whole staircase.
—Martin Luther King, Jr.

That will be a hard climb,
but we must get over the hill, nevertheless.
—Scarecrow, *The Wonderful Wizard of Oz* (1900)

Learn as You Go

You've got yourself the beginnings of a fire. It's not a huge blaze, but it's definitely generating some heat.

If you've ever started a fire before, you know it takes work to get it lit, keep it burning, and not let it get out of control. You don't just strike a match and suddenly have a stable flame. It takes some time.

Similarly, it's safe to say that less-than-perfect beginnings are to be expected in the early stage of your impact journey. Fires, like fingerprints, are never the same—and that rule applies to the unique expedition you've begun to embark upon, as well. You are your own guide, but the way forward isn't clearly marked. You're just simply putting one foot in front of the other, taking steps toward who-knows-where.

Why would anyone choose to go on a journey that is completely unpredictable, risky, and has no clear destination? Because Pull keeps calling to you, Passion has your heart on lockdown, and Courage has convinced you *this matters* enough to actually *do something*... even if it's messy and you have no idea *what* you're doing.

This is where you learn as you go. You let your instinct—formed by your values, past experiences, and maybe even some good old blind-faith—guide you. And if you realize you've started going in the wrong direction, you course-correct.

> *Pull keeps calling to you, Passion has your heart on lockdown, and Courage has convinced you this matters enough to actually do something.*

Sneak peek into your future: One day, you'll suddenly realize you're much more confident in the direction you've been heading. Why? Because you'll see how far you've come and recognize the cumulative progress is the result of every single step you've taken along the way. It's all had value, even the messy stuff.

Your fire is lit, so it's LFG time. (Let's Firing Go!) It won't be perfect—so you've just got to build while it burns.

It Can Be Messy at First

As the saying goes, you've got to start somewhere—but I had literally no idea what I was doing once my fire was lit and it was LFG time.

When I started my assistantship at the UCLA LGBT Campus Resource Center, I didn't know what I was capable of or how to be of help. And quite honestly, beyond my own myopic lens as a middle-class, gay, white male—who had countless blind spots—I didn't know much about the incredibly diverse community I was being called to support. What I did know was I carried a perspective forged through my lived experiences, a desire to understand others, and deep compassion etched into my heart, mind, and soul. Oh yeah, *and* that voice inside that kept insisting I *do something* in service of others.

I still remember my first day working there. I walked in, big smile on my face, headed to the intern desk and enthusiastically offered a "Hey, guys!" to the Women's Studies major seated there with a few of her friends.

Big smiles were not returned. "Do we look like guys to you?"

Oh, #*^@. What did I just say? What did I just do? I'm an idiot. That was apparently (clearly?) offensive. What was I thinking? What am I doing here? I'm already in over my head. This is too hard. I'm already the perpetrator—maybe even the enemy—amongst my own people. Screw this—I am *not* built to do this work!

Yep, all of those panicky thoughts began hammering inside my head. I remember fumbling afterward, holding onto my shame for the rest of the day (rest of my life?), trying desperately to make sense of her response. Was I being asked a serious question? Taught a lesson? Punished? Razzed? I'm still not sure, but fortunately that was the only time I messed up—it was all clear sailing from there.

Gosh, I wish that was the case!

In reality, those early days were terrifying. I'd often feel like I was walking on eggshells, worrying about what I was saying, how I was saying it, and who I was saying it to. It felt like a roller coaster filled with mess-ups, clean-ups, and learning while doing. This came along with:

- Stepping on toes
- Being told to stay in my lane
- Feeling like an imposter
- Feeling like I was bending over backwards, only to hear I didn't care enough or didn't "get it"

I frequently wanted to call it quits. Life was so much easier when I only had to worry about myself, how I saw the world, and what worked for me. Now, needing to monitor my language and actions constantly—for the sake of others who had different experiences and needs—felt exhausting. But even in those low points, the Pull was still there. Something deeper kept insisting *this matters* too much to quit.

Every stumble was painful and maddening, yet each one taught me something important if I allowed it to. And it was both rewarding and even liberating each time I began to "get it." Staying humble and resilient in service of something bigger than me, I found myself learning, my relationships growing, and my connection to humanity getting stronger.

To this day, in continuing to follow the Pull and live in my purpose, it's still messy and confusing at times. For instance, should I never say "Hey, guys" to a group of people again? But didn't I just see a woman walk up to her girlfriends and say it?? Is it sometimes a yes, sometimes a no???

Who knows—I most certainly don't have it all figured out. Language is imperfect, the work is imperfect, I am imperfect, and the world is imperfect.

Yes, sometimes the Pull to "throw in the towel" has felt strong, but the Pull to hold true to my values and keep going has remained stronger, because that inner voice keeps reminding me *this matters*. And every time I recognized that my actions were having a positive impact on others, I knew that was my signal to continue forward.

Sometimes the Pull to "throw in the towel" has felt strong, but the Pull to hold true to my values and keep going has remained stronger.

Warning: Potential Self-Sabotage Ahead

We all have to start somewhere; there's really no option but to build while it burns. Even those who make it look easy, do it in the public eye, or whom we just assume are so much braver than us likely still have to work through:

- Self-rejection: *I'll say "no" to myself before anyone else has a chance to.*
- Comparison trap: *I could never do it as well as others.*
- Anxiety of influence: *I have nothing new or of value to add.*
- Imposter syndrome: *I'm not qualified enough to do it.*
- Perfectionism paralysis: *I'm not even close to being ready.*

Do any of these common self-sabotage patterns resonate with you? Welcome to the club—we've all been there in one way or another. Heck, I've been delaying writing a book for over 15 years (and have documentation to prove it) . . . for all of those reasons!

Also, around 15 years ago, I met Jeanette Jennings and her then 11-year-old daughter Jazz at a conference called Creating Change. They were out there in the public eye, sharing their family's story and literally "creating change" in ways that seemed unimaginable to me. They were *special* and clearly much braver, more intentional, and more capable than the average person (and me, for sure), right? Well, I'll let Jeanette share her impact journey with you, so you can decide.

I Went with My Gut—*Jeanette Jennings*

My impact journey began with simply trying to get my daughter into kindergarten as herself. I went to the school and said, "I have a transgender daughter. She needs to go by female pronouns, dress like a girl, use the girls' restroom, and be referred to as Jazz." At first the school didn't want to speak to us at all. Then someone I knew suggested we go to the local press to put some pressure on the school to give us a meeting, and that's exactly what we did. Well, the local article then got picked up by New York City's *The Village Voice*, and from there ABC News' *20/20* tracked us down.

We were like, absolutely not—we're not putting our five-year-old on TV. We just wanted to get her into school. Well, the ABC News folk were the nicest people, and for ten months they wooed us—"There's nobody else out there like you, your story needs to be heard, it'll help other people." We finally said, "Okay, we'll do it—but you can't show our faces and we'll change our names." They said that wouldn't work—people needed to see Jazz to understand. My husband said, "We'll only do it if you give us Barbara Walters." They said absolutely. We were shocked. We really didn't intend to . . . we fell into it backwards . . . but we knew it was important, because other families were out there struggling, hiding behind closed doors. They needed to know they weren't alone.

From left: Jeanette Jennings, Barbara Walters, Greg Jennings, Jazz Jennings.

In the beginning there was nobody out there like us. This was back in 2000–2003; a parent's guide to supporting a transgender preschooler didn't exist. In my support group, I was the only one with a little kid like Jazz. I knew of no one else trying to support a transgender kindergartner. When we did the Barbara Walters piece, we got tossed into the limelight—just for Jazz's right to attend kindergarten as a girl. I wanted to be part of a community of parents. Once that piece came out, transgender kindergartners started to surface and more support groups popped up. That was the first sign that stepping forward—without a roadmap—was helping other families.

I was told about the Philadelphia Trans Wellness Conference. I went, and there were no kids there. I thought, "Where are all the trans kids?" The next year, we decided to throw a party for kids and spread the word, and dozens of kids showed up. It became a famous pool party for many years. One year, a teenager came up to me and said, "This is the first time I've ever gone swimming without a shirt on. You've changed my life. Thank you." We hugged, and I cried and he cried. I knew there was a huge impact.

I've also had letters from people who said, "My kid would not be alive today if it wasn't for you—your child and your story." I've had kids say they were literally ready to take their own lives but thought of Jazz and our family and didn't do it. Knowing we've saved at least one life makes my journey meaningful. We're making a difference.

It wasn't about doing media. It was sporadic—the first time when Jazz was six, then a revisit with Barbara Walters at age 12. We were in protective mode—all of the talk shows called, but we weren't going to put our kid on a couch to get questions from an audience, even when it was Oprah. We had to protect her. That was the most important thing.

By the time Jazz was 14, a lot of companies were coming to us wanting to do a show. We wanted to help people, but we were concerned about our family and our safety.

We sat Jazz down and asked, "Are you ready for something like this?" We wanted to make sure she was 100 percent on board, and she was. We were told our show, *I Am Jazz,* would probably only go one season. We ended up doing eight seasons; it just kind of snowballed.

In the beginning, we were nervous. We were scared. We didn't have clout. We're just us. But we didn't wait to feel ready—we moved because the purpose was clear.

The Jennings family. Top to bottom; left to right: Greg, Jeanette, Ari, Jazz, Sander and Griffen.

People think we're celebrities, but we really are not. We just share our lives about a topic that's important for people to understand, and then go back to being a regular family. I went from someone afraid to show my face on TV to someone who can stand up in front of hundreds or thousands and tell our story. I like being in the trenches and speaking on behalf of families that can't go public.

I can't talk about our journey without talking about David St. John. From the moment I met him, I fell in love with him—one of the finest people you'll ever meet. Without him there would have been no *I Am Jazz;* he was the foundation and the guiding light. In December 2024, he passed away from pancreatic cancer. When he was in hospice, a nurse taking care of him asked what he did for work. He told her he was the producer of *I Am Jazz.*

She started to cry and told him she had a transgender daughter and said, "If it wasn't for your show, I don't know where we'd be today." We made a difference together—it takes a village. It wasn't just our family; it was other people supporting us and surrounding us. *I Am Jazz* would not be *I Am Jazz* without David St. John.

We kind of just threw the first stone, and I didn't know at the time what was going to happen, but there's been a ripple effect—it's undeniable and I'm proud of that. And I have evolved—I found my voice as an advocate. I go with my gut. It's not always perfect, but it usually leads me in the right direction. It's passion, too—a drive to help other people and keep growing into a better version of myself. Jazz made me the best version of me in ways I never expected. No one plans for a transgender child; there wasn't a what-to-expect guide for that. We learn in real time, and we share what we learn so fewer families feel alone.

The Jennings with David St. John. From left: (back row) Greg, Sander, and Griffen; (front row) Jeanette, David, and Jazz.

I keep a sentence in the back of my mind: Courage doesn't mean you're not afraid—it means you choose to act despite fear. We were always afraid, but we knew we had to be courageous, to make a better life for Jazz and to make this world a better place.

We all have fear, but I think it's unhealthy to squash that drive when your gut's telling you to do something, or your mind's telling you that you should. I think ultimately you'll feel bad if you push that away and don't speak up.

You don't have to change the world or do a million things to have an impact. You can speak at your synagogue, join a support group, sit on a panel—tiny steps count. Your knowledge will benefit someone else, and you'll feel better for following your gut and going with your passion.

• • •

Connecting to Other Firestarters

Even for public figures like the Jennings family, who we assume might have it all figured out, embarking on an impact journey can feel scary and potentially even isolating. But I've got good news for you, Firestarter: You are not alone. Just as I learned when randomly meeting Jeanette years ago and staying connected ever since, there are other Firestarters all around you who value a strong support network.

Of course, not everyone is a Firestarter. Sure, lots of people feel a Pull, but not everyone has their internal fire fully lit and has the Courage and willingness to push through the messiness. These are attributes that make someone (you) special and will be sensed by other Firestarters. You might not even realize you have these shared traits at first, but if you sense a commonality and take the time to get to know someone a bit more, they'll very possibly show up.

That happened to me recently when I met my next door neighbors' daughter. After a few initial "Hi, how's your day going?" type interactions, we both sensed there might be value in continuing the conversation, so we decided to grab a coffee. This is when I got to learn more about Wendy Pollack: a three-time cancer survivor and former corporate executive who rebuilt her life after two stem cell transplants and severe burnout. Her own healing and self-discovery journey led her to Courageously launch BoldSoul Wellness. With the fire burning inside her, she is committed to empowering women to heal deeply, avoid burnout, and live vibrantly.

It's a Daily Practice—*Wendy Pollack*

I remember sitting on the balcony overlooking the water after a 12-hour workday, too exhausted to eat. On paper, I had it all—the dream corporate job, the high-ranking title, the relationship, the house with the view—but inside I felt numb, empty, disconnected, unfulfilled. That moment forced me to get radically honest about how I'd been suppressing emotions, numbing pain, and chasing success because it felt safer than facing what was unresolved within me. I knew something had to change.

Two weeks later, a conversation planted the seed for my journey overseas and, eventually, the birth of BoldSoul Wellness. Once I walked through that door, there was no going back.

When I launched my wellness business, I thought I'd already done the deep healing work. That first week proved otherwise. The moment I said yes to this path, every doubt surfaced. I was flooded with imposter syndrome—as if all the old mental programming tried to pull me back. I couldn't stay frozen, so I sat with those unraveled beliefs that weren't even mine—rooted in old conditioning, survival mode, systems never designed for women like me to thrive—and did the mindset work.

It didn't erase the fear, but it gave me tools to move through it. It would have been easier to shrink back to a corporate paycheck and hide behind the identity I'd built, but I chose courage.

I chose to believe that my story, my scars, my struggles, my softness were not weaknesses but my greatest qualifications. I had to trust myself more than I ever had, believe that even if my voice shook, it still mattered, and choose alignment over approval—not just for me, but for every woman who needed to hear it.

That choice doesn't happen once. Every day you wake up with a choice: predictable structure and stability, or the unknown, the unguaranteed, the soul-led mission that lights a fire in your belly. It's not a one-time mindset shift; it's a daily practice—evolving, recommitting, meeting yourself with compassion. Courage isn't loud here. It's quiet and consistent: choosing the unknown path again and again because your soul knows it's true.

The more I committed, the more I softened—listening to my body, trusting my intuition, leading with heart instead of hustle. I built a community where women take off their masks and are seen. The ripple keeps me going: Women who finally feel understood, cancer survivors who no longer feel alone, corporate women who say, "You gave me the permission I didn't know I needed." When one woman chooses to heal, it doesn't stop with her.

• • •

Let Your Pull Be Your Guide

Ever feel, even as a full-grown adult, like you're still the kid version of yourself—just trapped in an older body? Still trying to figure life out and wishing someone would show you the way? It's a hard pill to swallow when you realize you're all grown up and on your own, kid.

Like Wendy and Jeanette discovered, there's no roadmap to follow. You just need to trust your Pull, take the next imperfect step, and let your journey—and often, a change reAction—unfold. In the end, the only one with *your* answers is *you*.

One of the first rules of thumb I try to follow when coaching someone is to never tell them what I think they should do. Why? Because as each of us navigates our own life, there are countless factors at play that only we could possibly know. If you give someone a synopsis of a problem you're trying to solve and ask what they think you should do, I can almost guarantee you their answer won't hit the bullseye because ______________________ (fill in *allllll* the details they weren't aware of).

It's the same with your impact journey. Only *you* understand what brought you to the point of ignition when you decided to strike the match. Only *you* know the circumstances—working for or against you—in the situation you're facing. Only *you* are intimately familiar with the skills, talents, gaps, and emotions you're juggling that will shape the approach that works best for you. Sure, people will offer insights, opinions, and past experiences that might be useful to hear. But at the end of the day, *you* are the one in the driver's seat.

Hold true to your values, don't lose sight of your intention, and trust yourself and that fire inside you. Then know that even when things feel tough, it's all part of your unfolding (and maybe a bit messy) impact journey.

That said, having people in your corner is invaluable as you persist. One person who played a pivotal support role during a major transition in my impact journey is Mason Dunn—an LGBTQ+ and reproductive rights advocate and educator who's held high-level leadership roles and helped advance trans-inclusive laws and policies. Mason knows how fierce the headwinds can be—inside and out—which is why he advises trusting in yourself and staying rooted in community as you build while it burns.

Don't Do It Alone—*Mason Dunn*

Some of the hardest moments I've faced have come from struggling with imposter syndrome. I often feel like I'm not good enough, not smart enough, not experienced enough . . . and those feelings can spiral into self-doubt, fear, and indecision. In social justice work, the pressure to be the "perfect" advocate is intense, and the harshest, most hurtful criticisms often come from within the movement itself.

When my imposter syndrome flares up, part of me wants to walk away from this work. In those moments—when strangers' voices echo the lies my inner critic already whispers—I lean on my friends and allies. Without that circle of support, I would have let imposter syndrome stop me a hundred times over. I've learned that reaching out—whether for advice, encouragement, or just a kind word—can make all the difference. In those moments of fear and burnout, I turn to my chosen family. They listen to my frustrations and fears, remind me of my worth, and help me find the confidence to keep going. I'm deeply grateful for them—I know I wouldn't be where I am today without their love and support.

Never do this work alone. Build a community, or a chosen family, around you that can help you through the hard times, and celebrate with you in the good times. Never be too proud to ask for help—trust me, I'm guilty of this far too often, and I always regret it.

Success doesn't follow a script. It may not look the way you imagined, or feel as big as it should, but that doesn't diminish the work it took to get there. Take pride in the effort, no matter how it's recognized. And celebrate your wins on your own terms. Don't wait for someone else to mark the occasion. Throw your own party, and surround yourself with the people who truly matter.

• • •

REFLECTING ON ONGOING PULL

- Write your Pull mantra: one sentence your inner voice says that reminds you why *this matters*, even when things feel shaky.
- What's "good enough to move forward" right now? Name two ways it might be messy and one reason you'll do it anyway.
- Name one internal headwind (e.g., self-talk) and one external headwind (e.g., logistics). For each, write the specific help you'll request and who you'll ask.
- Write a two-sentence affirmation note you'll read when doubt spikes. Include an example from the past that proves you can do hard things.
- Pick one micro-win you can complete in the next 48 hours that proves progress without perfection. How will you celebrate when it's complete?

Want to see a clip from Tom's conversation with Jeanette Jennings?

Scan the QR Code below or visit www.thenextlevelimpact.com/firestarter-videos

Add Fuel to Your Fire

You have to go the way your blood beats.
If you don't live the only life you have, you won't
live some other life—you won't live any life at all.
—James Baldwin

You people with hearts have something to guide you.
—Tin Man, *The Wonderful Wizard of Oz* (1900)

This Journey Requires Stamina

When it comes to Pull, you *build while it burns* because the voice inside says you have to. When it comes to Passion, you *add fuel to your fire* because you want to.

This isn't about triaging burnout. It's about continuing to follow your heart and sustaining—and even increasing—the Passion that helped launch you on this journey in the first place.

The journey you're on requires stamina. To keep going with sustained interest and compounding impact, you have to stay intrigued and motivated. Any good leader knows the only way to get someone to truly put their best foot forward is to make sure they really care. Well, *you* are leading *yourself* on this journey, so to stay energized and put your best foot forward, you have to keep feeding your fire.

Finding ways to "fill your cup" while doing the hard work is both essential and exhilarating. It's not indulgence; it's energy. That might feel counterintuitive at first, but if every step feels heavy, you won't stick with it. I'm not talking about sneaking away for a relaxing massage or overdue vacation (although those can of course be great energizers). I'm talking about identifying renewable energy that connects to the work: partnering with amazing people, trying new approaches, experiencing personal growth, and—most gratifying of all—witnessing the impact of your efforts firsthand.

Firestarter, your flame is meant to burn bright. It fuels you and can ignite a change reAction when others are drawn to the heat you're radiating. For all these reasons and more, it's essential to keep adding fuel to your fire.

Feel the Heat, Feed My Fire

My impact journey has taught me to try new things all the time. It isn't restlessness; it's my deliberate way to keep my Passion alive. I've found myself feeding my fire with ongoing learning, taking on bigger responsibilities, attacking more complex issues, connecting into new networks, and the occasional reset. I try to keep my heat sensors on and follow the warmth, adjusting as needed to keep the flame strong.

Continuing to move toward the unknown can make things feel a bit unsteady—maybe even scary. But keep in mind, there can be profound benefit in moving toward what scares you. It's allowed me to follow my heart, grow my impact, and keep my fire burning for over two decades, even as things change shape.

Here are some ways I've added fuel that might spark ideas for you:

Expand the Focus

LGBTQ+ issues drew me into my impact journey, but I quickly realized that being truly effective requires serving the diverse community holistically. Intersectional issues connected to race, religion, ability, nationality, and more are inseparable from the work. Thinking beyond gender and sexuality alone was both necessary and energizing, and I felt my Passion build as I started viewing everything through that wider diversity, equity, and inclusion lens.

I sought out ways to expand my capabilities. One of the earliest opportunities was by raising my hand to chair a newly formed Social Justice Leadership Initiative in addition to my LGBTQ+ center responsibilities. I had to learn fast, felt pressure to prove myself, and things got messy more than once—but it paid off. Continuing to identify even more ways to widen my scope added serious fuel to my fire.

→ Same mission, expanded focus = more fuel.

Change the Setting

After a decade working on university campuses, various micro-moments indicated I was ready to take a sharp turn on my impact journey. That led to a macro-movement: shifting from higher education to the nonprofit sector with my skills, knowledge, and Passion in tow.

The values and mission stayed aligned, but my responsibilities as a leader changed significantly. I now had to mobilize volunteers to expand the organization's impact, craft strategy, think persuasively to influence policymakers and voters, push to pass laws to improve lives, and inspire donors and corporate partners to sustain the work financially.

Over time, I realized I was most energized by the strategic and inspirational work, but the constant need to fundraise was eclipsing what fueled my Passion.

I was also fascinated by the surge of interest in diversity, equity, and inclusion among some of the corporate sponsors I was partnering with. They had a need for more in-house expertise, and I felt the heat rise in me yet again. This led me to another macro-movement: moving from the nonprofit world over to corporate. This change in setting allowed me to support organizations whose inclusion-related values aligned with mine, focus on the work that energized me most, and stay intrigued by fresh approaches, goals, and impact.

→ Same values, different settings = more fuel.

Solve It at the Source

For many impact-driven people, the work starts at the interpersonal level. Being able to provide one-on-one help is incredibly rewarding, but over time it can become emotionally draining. You also begin to notice patterns that often tie unique challenges to common root causes. For instance, I would see diverse individuals repeatedly overlooked or misjudged. While I wanted to support them all individually, I also wanted to wave a magic wand and resolve the dynamics that caused these universal problems in the first place.

I felt a strong Pull to better understand how organizations and systems work—and how to change them for the greater good—which led me to continue my education in organizational leadership. It also led me to facilitate training sessions and workshops, teach college courses, and speak publicly to educate and raise awareness—because prevention-first beats repair-later. Witnessing people's real-time shifts in awareness and eagerness to be agents of positive change felt like watching change reActions unfold right in front of me. I could see next-level impact taking shape, and my Passion soared.

→ Getting to the root of the issues = more fuel.

Ignite Leaders, Amplify Impact

Having served as a leader in multiple capacities has taught me how to drive meaningful impact. I also realized through these experiences how much I love supporting other driven leaders and Firestarters. Stepping into consulting and mentoring felt natural—a way to share what my experience has taught me and support others as they chart their own path. From there, coaching was an obvious next step: partnering with people to surface their own answers, shape a plan, and reach their goals.

For me, nothing beats watching someone connect their Pull, Passion, and Courage, strike the match, and make an impact in their own unique way. Few things are more gratifying than knowing I played even a small part in that journey.

→ From leading change to empowering leaders = more fuel.

Same Fire, Fresh Fuel

Each purposeful pivot along a connected path kept me aligned, added fuel, and made the flame burn brighter as my impact reached further.

The same is true of my fellow Firestarter, Raffi Freedman-Gurspan. Her impact journey has led her into some of the most visible and influential arenas in public service—from national advocacy organizations to the State House to the White House (twice). Her résumé is extraordinary, but what fuels her isn't titles or prestige—it's being able to weave her identities, values, and experiences into one purpose: ensuring marginalized communities are heard, included, and protected.

Fueled by Advocacy and Service—*Raffi Freedman-Gurspan*

I have always understood what it is like to be misunderstood, to be judged for an immutable characteristic in an unfair way, and to be made to feel different and not part of a community. As I grew older and accepted myself for who I am—and the multiple layers that I am—I recognized I wanted to commit my life to helping other people and to advocate with those seeking change, justice, and equality. For me, that started with the LGBTQ+ community, of which I am a part, but it has since extended to international adoptees, Latino/POC (People of Color) communities, Indigenous communities, people living with disabilities, and gender equality.

Coming out in 8th grade, first as a gay boy and later, in college, as a transgender woman, and being accepted and supported by family and friends, had a profound impact on my trajectory. I came of age during the marriage equality fight in Massachusetts, at a time when transgender people were truly coming out of the shadows. I learned I was not alone, but also that I had it relatively "well" growing up, and I wanted to make sure kids like me were afforded the same rights and safety I had. That instinct—to make things better for the next person—has guided every step since.

As an international adoptee whose birth mother is Central American Indigenous (Lenca), I have always felt connected not only to the Latino community but also to the Native American / First Nations communities in the US. It's why, years later while working on voting rights, I pushed to support Indigenous communities in North and South Dakota. I advocated hard that we provide training, pro bono, to these Indigenous community members because, from a moral/ethical perspective, their voices matter. If we weren't assisting them, how could we claim to be doing the important work of empowering local communities? Not only did the maps marginally improve for the Native communities, but it was really the first time either legislature in Pierre and Bismarck had so many Native American community members testify regarding the maps. It was a proud moment, and I knew we had made a difference in the lives of these Indigenous peoples.

I often credit the incredible teachers and mentors I had along the way, along with my parents, who taught me to be brave, to not give up, and to believe in myself. That came in extremely helpful when I was invited to serve in the White House as the Outreach and

Recruitment Director for Presidential Personnel. I hesitated, unsure if I was ready, but my father said, "Raffi, it's the White House . . . they believe you can do the job." I said yes and became the first openly transgender staffer to work at the White House. I've since had the honor of serving as a presidential appointee to the US Holocaust Memorial Council for five years, a presidential appointee as the Principal Deputy Director of Public Engagement at the US Department of Transportation for three years, and today I'm a governor appointee to the Commonwealth of Massachusetts.

All of these opportunities, along with many others, have allowed me to continuously build on my passion and commitment to be of service to others and to advocate with those seeking change, justice, and equality. It's hard to imagine ever not being involved in the betterment of our society. I was mentored by people who had worked hard to keep people alive during the HIV/AIDS crisis in the 1980s and by community organizers who rallied for worker and immigrant rights in the 1990s, and I've seen the fruits of national organizers' efforts in getting the Affordable Care Act passed. I recognize that history is an important messenger to help us make decisions for the future, and that I have a responsibility to the next generation of leaders who will lead this country.

• • •

Inspirational Fuel

As Raffi and I have both learned, turning to others for inspiration and motivation is a powerful way to add fuel to your fire.

Hopefully you already have people in your life who can offer this type of support—through your cause, family and social circle, aligned organizations, or broader network. But if not, know that people like this can still appear along your path when you least expect it. Either way, when you feel someone else's heat, move toward it and see where it leads.

This happened to me with Deborra-lee Furness. We shared an amazing mutual friend, Brian Walsh, who reached out one day and said, "Tom, I need to introduce you to Deb. I feel like you two have a lot in common—as adoptive parents and in other ways—and I want you to connect." It was mid-2020: COVID had just hit, I'd lost my job, and my fire was running low. Walshie had a sixth sense—and a gift for spotting something special in people (having launched the careers for some of the biggest Australian icons out there[1])—so saying yes was a no-brainer.

From our first conversation, I felt real heat with Deb. That connection led me to join the board of directors for one of the two nonprofits she founded, focused on another Passion of mine: adoption. Every conversation since has fueled me to follow my heart, be brave, and be willing to try something new.

Our dear friend Brian has since left this earth and is now an angel above, but the fuel he added to my fire through that introduction lives on. And now, I'll let Deb inspire you.

---

[1] See the documentary on Brian Walsh's legacy: *The Great Entertainer*, Borce Damcevski, director (2025), https://www.imdb.com/title/tt38348640/.

We All Need Purpose—*Deborra-lee Furness*

I think we all need a purpose. What gives us our purpose is what our passions are and what we're good at. We have natural abilities, natural gifts, and we feel good about ourselves when we're good at something—so that leads us toward our purpose. Our gifts and passions are like a roadmap.

But as they say, we make a plan and God laughs, because uncertainty is what we are made of, and every day is uncertain. One of my purposes was a surprise: being an advocate for adoption and children in foster care.

It came organically. I fell upon this because we went to an adoption meeting in Australia many years ago and I saw how badly run it was. There were about 30 families in the room who wanted to adopt a child and make them part of their family, but the person speaking was so negative about the process. There was no energy, creativity, or motivation to make the system work. I was appalled at the lack of organisation and urgency required to ensure a safe home for these children. I remember thinking how vulnerable children need the grown-ups to advocate for them, and surely the way we treat our most vulnerable citizens represents who we are as a people—but it was clearly very low on the political agenda.

We moved to America and adopted there—which was a much easier process. But the question stayed with me: Why was adoption made so incredibly hard in Australia?

We were public figures, and when I spoke out about the situation to a journalist, it ended up on the front page. Suddenly it was "Deborra-lee and her adoption advocacy group," which, of course, there was none—just me going, "This is BS, what's going on?"

People from the community started coming to me and asking me to keep talking. So I kept talking because I hate injustice—especially when it's an injustice to a child. I once heard Robin Williams say that he had sadness as a little boy, and because of that he could have empathy for other people who felt that, and he wanted to take away everyone's pain. That resonated with me. I was an only child and went to boarding school at a young age, which made me very empathetic. I think we all have a need to feel we belong.

It did take courage to keep going, because when I spoke out I was attacked. There was an anti-adoption culture in Australia based on the country's ugly history with adoption. People tried to put us up against the Stolen Generations of Aboriginal children—which is not the same; those babies *were* stolen. And in recent decades there had also been young birth mothers who'd been forced to relinquish their babies. So there was such a negative outlook and a lot of pushback. I had to sit with myself, look at the facts, and ask, "We're trying to find homes for children—am I wrong in advocating that every child should belong in a loving family?" Late at night I'd try to respond to people being nasty, to educate myself and allay fears. What made me keep going was looking at a child's face and thinking, "I'm aware—and if I do nothing, that's negligence."

I also felt the responsibility because people would see me as an adoptive mother and go, "We'd love to adopt, but we can't, and it's not fair." They were right: It's not fair, and I wanted to help. Like most of us human beings, we want to be of service. That's how we're wired—to be of service.

I remember being on a talk show, and just before we went on air the interviewer leaned over and whispered, "I'm adopted." I went, "Oh," and he said, "But no one knows." It made me crazy. There was such a stigma around adoption—shame around being adopted. Part of the work became putting the conversation out there so people could own it: "I'm adopted, and this is my story . . ." without shame or fear of judgement.

It was never like "I'm going to start a movement." It was a very organic process—it was like I was walking along, and suddenly there was a crowd—and then we formalized it. We kept advocating. It was hard then and it's still really hard. You attract people to keep you buoyant and stay on your path and focused on your mission.

The work kept expanding. Access to adoption, yes—and ending the stigma. And then came the issue of trauma—any child separated from their birth family has ongoing trauma. We've got to talk about trauma-informed care. Doctors aren't trained in trauma—we treat symptoms without asking, "What's going on in your life?" I will continue to advocate for trauma-informed care, because without it we are not supporting these children who have traversed so many difficulties in their young lives.

Then there are the systems. Right now in Australia, the system doesn't know what to do, so we're seeing some young children in the government care system who are being housed in motels and supervised by a revolving door of unaccredited agency employees who aren't trained in trauma-informed care of children. And in other countries, there are orphanages—and of course sometimes there does need to be somewhere for children to be cared for—but children don't thrive in orphanages, and in some cases there's corruption that leads to trafficking, and many of those kids are inserted into modern slavery. So then you push on legislation, you keep the conversation going—you write, you make partnerships, you raise awareness—because if you don't put it on the table, nothing's going to shift. As a community we need to continue to seek the best possible solutions and outcomes for these children.

It's systemic. The longer a child isn't in a permanent family, the more issues there are.

I'm kept motivated because there's always something: You think you've solved a problem and—whoops—there's another one. The tentacles keep reaching and we keep going.

I believe the universe is running the show. I might think I'm running the show, but the universe is going to place obstacles or opportunities in my way that I must take advantage of or utilize to move the needle. I feel that I am used by the universe to do what I do.

Along the way, I had to learn sustainability. Boundaries are vital. "No" is a complete sentence. You've got to know your capacity or you'll burn out. I used to people-please; I've learned it isn't good for me or the other person. It's like Legos—if you pull out one piece, the whole thing can fall apart, so you fit the right pieces together.

Know your gifts and bring what you're good at. I know my gifts—I'm a juggler—mother, artist, writer, actor, director. But start throwing numbers at me and I'm taking a nap—so I delegate the parts that would zap my joy. Partner with people who complement you. Don't force yourself into roles that drain your joy—when you do that, things fall apart. If you're doing what you're supposed to do, it should fill you with vitality. Self-care is number one; the stronger and healthier you are, the more you can do.

There's only going to be change and action if you take yourself out of your comfort zone, and you have to. That's where the biggest growth happens—when you are uncomfortable. It doesn't have to be big or dramatic; people think it has to be huge. It can be a simple, simple step. If you have an intention, you take a simple step, and then—as it did with me—the universe takes over and leads you to something else, and then to something else. But you have to have the courage to take the step.

> *There's only going to be change and action if you take yourself out of your comfort zone. . . . That's where the biggest growth happens—when you are uncomfortable.*

Purpose, for me, sits under an umbrella that encompasses creativity. Even the organisations I created—that was creativity when asking myself, "How do we help? How do we create something?" I love to create, to bring people together, to build community. Creativity feeds everything else I do.

I love that Billie Eilish song, "What Was I Made For?" It's beautiful and it's true. We always go, "What's my purpose?" I still ask, "What is my purpose? What am I supposed to do? What drives me?" I'm still learning, but I know love is the overall thing for me. I always try to lead with love and live truly in my authentic self.

• • •

Firestarter Check-Up

As we see with Deborra-lee, identifying what drives you and building sustainability is essential, because some days the heat runs high and other days it doesn't.

If you pay close enough attention, you'll also be able to identify what has been adding fuel to your fire and what's been draining your energy.

When you find yourself having those WTF (where's the fire?) moments, a Firestarter Check-Up can help you get clear on what is (and isn't) feeding your fire—clarity you'll need if you plan to stay on this journey for the long haul. As you go through a Firestarter Check-Up, you can consider things like:

- What tasks do you love/hate, and do they align with your skills/Passion?
- Who are you surrounding yourself with?
- How is the information you're consuming (including social media) affecting your mood and mindset?
- Are you allowing yourself to celebrate wins . . . even the small ones?
- Are you able to lean into self-care to give you that short-term boost you might need?

You can do a Firestarter Check-Up at both the micro-moment and macro-movement level. If you're using an Impact Journal, I recommend doing it there.

EXERCISE: FIRESTARTER CHECK-UP

TODAY
(Micro-Moment)

Heat Gauge: How Are You Doing?

☐ Burning hot (bright/steady)
- Details: ____________________
  ____
- Action Needed: ____________________
  ____

☐ Not so hot (cooling/at risk)
- Details: ____________________
  ____
- Action Needed: ____________________
  ____

Fuel Audit: What Does Your Fire Need?

- Adds fuel to my fire (+): ____________________
- Dims my flame (-): ____________________
- Next log to add: ____________________
- Leaks to seal: ____________________

EXERCISE: FIRESTARTER CHECK-UP

THIS STAGE OF YOUR JOURNEY
(Macro-Movement)

Heat Gauge: How Are You Doing?

☐ Burning hot (bright/steady)
- Details: ______________________________
  ____
- Action Needed: ______________________________
  ____

☐ Not so hot (cooling/at risk)
- Details: ______________________________
  ____
- Action Needed: ______________________________
  ____

Fuel Audit: What Does Your Fire Need?

- Adds fuel to my fire (+): ______________________________
- Dims my flame (-): ______________________________
- Next log to add: ______________________________
- Leaks to seal: ______________________________

You've come a long way, Firestarter. Keep adding fuel to your fire so you can continue burning strong—and remember: When your Passion radiates, it draws people in; that's how a change reAction ignites.

REFLECTING ON ONGOING PASSION

- If you follow the heat right now, where does it point you?
- How are you able to tie your natural abilities to your impact journey?
- What's one quick way and one substantial way you could add fuel to your fire?
- What's one thing that dims your flame—and what action will you take to counter it?
- Who has caused a change reAction in you, inspiring you to burn brighter—and how can you let them know this?

Want to see a clip from Tom's conversation with Deborra-lee Furness?

Scan the QR Code below or visit
www.thenextlevelimpact.com/firestarter-videos

Let It Roar

I raise up my voice—not so that I can shout,
but so that those without a voice can be heard.
—Malala Yousafzai

You have plenty of courage, I am sure.
All you need is confidence in yourself.
—The Wizard to Cowardly Lion,
The Wonderful Wizard of Oz (1900)

Leading with Courage

You've been navigating yourself down this path for a while now. You've gotten more comfortable—your strides are longer, the direction feels more obvious, and you're more familiar with the ongoing heat you've been generating.

Suddenly you realize something—you have not been alone. A number of others have joined you at different stages of this journey, and many are now following you. Being followed can be scary. But it can also be powerful, because you know there's strength in numbers.

Directionally, it's clear you're no longer just steering yourself along—others are looking to you for direction. They're putting their trust in you because they think you know where you're going.

And you *are* now much more familiar with the landscape you're navigating, which means you *do* have valuable directions to offer others. They want your guidance—they need it.

This journey is no longer merely about following your Pull toward whichever way your heart tells you to go next. Now it's also about using your voice so others can follow your lead . . . and you being willing to take new risks along the way. The load you're carrying is heavier now—and you can feel it.

So the real question is this, Firestarter: Are you ready to lead with Courage, unleash your inner lion, and let it roar?

We All Have Potential to Roar

Every one of us has the potential to be brave, to lead, and to let our voice—and our fire—roar. It won't look the same for everyone, but regardless of age, communication style, or "readiness," our impact grows the moment we decide to see ourselves as leaders.

Case in point: Jazz Jennings. In chapter 4, you read her mom Jeanette's story about diving into unknown territory and building while her fire burned. Jazz has been the center point of that same journey for almost two decades—since she was six. If anyone shows us how to be ourselves and find the Courage to lead, it's Jazz.

Fear Is Natural, but Truth Is Stronger—*Jazz Jennings*

Since I was so young when I began my impact journey, I didn't fully grasp the weight of it at the time, but I knew that being open about who I was could help others feel less alone.

One of the earliest turning points was when my family and I did the *20/20* interview with Barbara Walters. I was only six years old, but even then, I could sense that sharing my truth had the power to open hearts and minds. I have to stress that my parents made sure I was comfortable sharing my life on TV. I know that if I was scared or nervous, they never would have proceeded.

Barbara Walters and Jazz, 2007.

That *20/20* interview in 2007 was groundbreaking, and it opened a powerful new chapter in my life. By sharing my story, I helped show the world that transgender children exist . . . and that we deserve love, respect, and acceptance. Many people had never seen a trans child before, and that visibility challenged their assumptions. It sparked empathy, shifted perspectives, and helped plant the seeds for greater understanding. That moment set a tone for change, proving that even the smallest voice can inspire compassion and open hearts.

When I first spoke publicly about being transgender, I was just 11 years old, standing in a ballroom before a thousand people, including A-list celebrities. I was terrified; I feared rejection and judgement. My heart raced, my hands trembled, but I knew that visibility mattered . . . not just for me, but for every child who felt unseen or unheard. I found courage in purpose, realizing that staying silent would help no one. When I finished, the room rose in a standing ovation. In that moment, fear transformed into pride, and I understood the power of

From left: Emily Mears, Jazz, and Tom at the Creating Change Conference, 2011.

using my voice to inspire hope and spark change.

I realized others were looking to me for guidance when families began reaching out after my interviews and TV appearances, sharing how my story gave them hope. Parents of transgender children thanked my family and me for helping them feel less alone . . . many had never known another trans youth before. It was deeply humbling to see how simply living my truth could shine a light for others. Even as a child, I felt the weight and beauty of that impact. It awakened in me a profound responsibility to lead with honesty, compassion, and the courage to keep showing up as myself.

> *It was deeply humbling to see how simply living my truth could shine a light for others. . . . I felt the weight and beauty of that impact.*

As I got older, the decision to continue sharing my journey—through interviews, public speaking, and ultimately our TV show *I Am Jazz*—became a calling, and our visibility was desperately needed. There still wasn't a lot of transgender representation in the media, let alone trans kids. We felt that if our journey could create change, inspire acceptance, save a life, or shift someone's understanding, then being vulnerable was absolutely worth it. We really wanted to help normalize what it means to be trans and show that every family, at its core, is built on love. So, when the letters and messages started pouring in from families around the world thanking us, and trans youth saying they felt seen for the first time and inspired on their own journeys, I realized this was so much bigger than me and my family.

Even though I try to live a pretty normal life—I hang out with friends and family, go to Harvard, binge-watch TV—there are definitely times I wish I could just live quietly, like any other young person, without the weight of being seen as a "spokesperson." But then I remind myself why I shared my story in the first place: to help others and make them feel less alone. It can be overwhelming at times, but knowing that my visibility can make a difference is what keeps me going, even when I long for that quiet.

Jazz at Harvard, 2025.

I think my purpose has always remained the same: I've always aspired to make a difference, to speak out to empower the trans community, and to inform those who wish to learn more about transgender people. I achieve this by creating awareness and spreading love and acceptance. How I do it has definitely changed over time—I've learned to be more flexible, to slow down when I need to, and to trust that even the smaller, quieter moments can still make a difference. My advocacy tends to ebb and flow depending on where I am in life. Sometimes

I'm out there speaking at events and rallies. Other times, I'm using social media or working through TV and storytelling to share my message. Each outlet has its own power, and I've learned that impact doesn't always have to be loud to be meaningful.

It's heartbreaking to see the world moving backwards when it comes to transgender rights and acceptance. Every day, our existence is politicized, and that kind of hatred can weigh heavily on your heart. But for me, protecting my well-being and my sense of self comes from holding on to love . . . love for who I am, love for my community, and love for my family. My family has always been my safe place. In a world that sometimes feels determined to erase us, my family reminds me that I am whole, worthy, and enough just as I am. We lean on each other, and that bond gives us strength to face the ugliness with compassion instead of hate. I won't pretend it's easy . . . some days it feels overwhelming . . . but I refuse to let the negativity define me.

Leadership, to me, means continuing to evolve while empowering the next generation to step into their voices. It's also about service, impact, and authenticity. My journey is ongoing, and I see limitless possibilities to spark change. While advocacy will always be at the heart of what I do, I hope to expand into mentoring, storytelling, and creative expression through art and media. I want to create spaces, both physical and emotional . . . where people feel seen, safe, and celebrated for who they are. My goal is to uplift voices that are too often silenced and help others find strength in their truth. I hope to inspire lasting change that continues to ripple outward long after I've spoken.

To anyone feeling that inner pull, fear is a natural part of the journey, but your truth is stronger. When you lead with love for yourself and stand up for what you believe in, courage will follow. Your voice matters! So, even if you help just one person by being true to who you are and sharing your story, that impact is real and meaningful. That alone makes it worth it. So, hold on to your truth, be brave, and trust that being authentic is enough to create the life you deserve.

• • •

Determined to Move Mountains

Jazz's story is a perfect example of what a change reAction looks like: being brave enough to live and lead authentically, which encourages others to step forward themselves.

Most Firestarters don't begin their impact journey as young as Jazz did—although the micro-moments that formed those initial sparks can often show up early. Case in point: Renée Leigh, CEO of Deborra-lee Furness's organization, Adopt Change.

Renée felt a very specific Pull since she was a child, but it wasn't until adulthood that she unexpectedly stepped into her role as a leader and force for change. Over the past decade, she's become a nationally recognized advocate in Australia who uses her voice and platform to help thousands of children in need.

As a former board member and now her coach, I've witnessed the bravery and leadership that Renée already had continue to deepen, year after year. I'm so inspired by her Courageous determination to move mountains for change, and I'm sure you will be inspired, as well.

I've Learned to Use My Voice—*Renée Leigh*

Since I was a child, I've wanted to help children who were suffering—especially those not living with their parents. I'm not even sure where that very early, very strong pull came from. But later in life, as an adult, I saw firsthand what it looked like for a child in Australia who couldn't live with their parents—not knowing where they'd sleep that night or where their next meal would come from—and I knew I had to do something.

I was working in a communications company I part-owned, but I felt a strong and growing urge to totally shift gears and drive change in the child protection system.

To my benefit or detriment, across my life I have often felt a pull to do something and would dive all in and figure out how to navigate it after I was already knee-deep. There have been nay-sayers, advising me against various pursuits. Someone close to me laughed at me when I said I wanted to positively change the child protection system in Australia. Needless to say, it didn't stop me. Instead, I listened to a friend who asked, "Who do you need to meet? Who does what you want to do?"

My answer was simple: Deborra-lee Furness. I truly admired her for her role in this space. So I reached out to the organisation she founded . . . and several months later, I found myself in the CEO seat, running it and in pursuit of finding more family homes, stability, and healing from trauma for the children in care.

Almost ten years in, I have learned to use my voice even more authentically, to elevate the needs of children who are often treated as voiceless, and to be part of the drive for improvements. It has been important for me to remember the individuals behind the statistics so that I speak with conviction and pursue results. After years of being vocal about the issues in media and in government meetings, the real encouragement has come from seeing the changes: bans on children being housed in motels with shiftworkers; increases to support for carer families; improvements to legislation, policy, and practice. Knowing that our work has opened new homes for children, supported those families, and engaged young people who have experienced living in foster care to have a better future continues to remind me this has been worth it.

Along the journey, I have sat in government meetings where I've been asked what was needed to solve a problem and to make change. The discussions I have been part of and changes I've helped influence have had me pinching myself. Over time, my responses in media interviews moved from "correct answers" to passionate statements and pleas about what needs to happen to bring about change. There are differing views in Australia when it comes to alternative homes for children, but over time I have seen more people willing to sit at the same table to collaborate on ways forward, and minds were changed where needed.

The people around me have been a huge part of my journey. It's powerful to meet those with lived experience and have it shape direction and conversations. And I'm so proud of the team I work alongside.

Our culture has evolved to collectively pursuing the seemingly impossible, all in the name of supporting children and families.

The work takes a huge amount of emotional energy, and there are times where it can feel like too much. A night's sleep usually resets me . . . along with the knowledge that the problem is not yet solved, so while I still have my fire burning, I will keep going.

There are thousands of children in Australia who don't have homes, their voices heard, or their needs met. I, however, have had the privilege of being able to use my voice since I was a young (and feisty) child. Over time, I've grown even more confident when using my voice, fueled by a clear mission and purpose. I have learned to lean into it . . . to stop diluting it and to become unapologetic in speaking authentically.

There is a reason I have a voice and "fight" within me, and I intend to arrive at the end of my life knowing I have used it in pursuit of what I believe is important.

• • •

Trust in Yourself

When it comes to my own leadership—and leaders like Renée who I have the privilege of supporting—one mantra rises above the rest: Trust in yourself. When fear or doubt creeps in, you can never be any more than you are—and that's OK, because you are enough.

Two high-stakes micro-moments tested this for me. In both situations, I chose to trust in myself and lead authentically, from the heart.

Spotlight Shining

It was the night of the annual fundraising gala for the nonprofit I was leading. The time had come for me to address the audience, and I stepped up to the podium with a swarm of butterflies going wild in my stomach. As Executive Director, I needed to give a keynote powerful enough to secure sufficient funding for the year ahead.

Moments earlier, we'd played a personal video from Lady Gaga congratulating her mother and Born This Way Foundation co-founder Cynthia Germanotta, who was our honoree. CEOs, government officials, sports team owners, a freaking Kennedy, and my own mother were somewhere among the 600 guests—but under the blinding spotlight I couldn't make out a single face.

I understood there was no way I could deliver a message perfectly tailored for all. It would be received differently by the fiercely committed constituents, wealthy donors, worn-down activists, event-hopping politicians, and the amazing woman who raised me. So with nerves rattling, I made a choice: Instead of focusing on everyone else, I needed to trust myself—my experience, my knowledge, my values, and my truth—and let the words flow from my heart. By this point, I had been sharing versions of my message for years, in different ways and to different ears.

Yes, it was scary to do then, just like it can still be scary now. But we exceeded our fundraising goal that night, so I guess I can say trusting in myself paid off.

It's a big shift, going from the emerging Firestarter who's just trying to figure things out to the Firestarter everyone thinks has it all figured out. Little secret: You never have it all figured out. But the more things you've seen, approaches you've tried, recoveries you've made, and conversations you've had, the more prepared you are for whatever comes next.

Oh, and as far as those butterflies? Sure, there are fewer over time. And yes, you get more used to them. But just know that they'll likely never be gone completely. Why? Because you're human. It's been well documented that even OG Firestarters . . . I'm talking Mahatma Gandhi, Mother Teresa, the Dalai Lama . . . never stopped getting butterflies. (Note: I completely made that up.)

> *If your fire is burning strong, simply trust in yourself, lean into Courage, and lead from your heart.*

The point is, impact-driven work is never easy, and can definitely feel scary. So just remember: If your fire is burning strong, simply trust in yourself, lean into Courage, and lead from your heart.

The Final Hurdle

While my first example of "trusting myself and leading authentically" unfolded under a spotlight, the second played out in a more personal setting. I was a finalist to lead diversity, equity, and inclusion at a global corporation—an opportunity that aligned perfectly with my Pull—but there were a number of hurdles I had to clear if they were to choose me.

The search had dragged on for nearly six months—it was so important they selected the right leader who could meet the role's requirements, organization's needs, and CEO's vision.

After clearing 15 interview conversations (yes, you read that right), it was time for #16—with the CEO. The recruiter gave me blunt advice for this final 20-minute test: "Be yourself . . . just steer clear of anything potentially too advanced or controversial . . . you know, stuff like 'white privilege' or 'unconscious bias.'"

To quote the great Cher Horowitz from *Clueless*: "As if!"

First off, white privilege and unconscious bias "too advanced"? That's the 101 stuff. My experience has taught me that if either of those terms feels new or threatening to someone, that's a prime opportunity to discuss these important concepts in a way that *doesn't* feel threatening and instead invites them into the discussion of "how we can make this world a better place for *everyone*."

On top of that, even if I played it safe and passed the final hurdle, there's no way I'd then be willing (or able) to take the role and not lead authentically. I refuse to compromise my values or dilute my approach toward impact. If I walked in as anyone but myself, I'd lose integrity and effectiveness. I hadn't come this far to backtrack or dim my fire.

So there I was, logging into Zoom, butterflies a-flutterin' and mind racing. How could I not address the privileges I've been afforded to get to this point? Or the obstacles I have and have not had to overcome, that shape not only who I am, but also the lens through which I view the world and how I approach the work?

As the CEO logged on, I weighed the potential risk—but equal importance—of outing myself in terms of how my lived experience as a queer person Pulled me into this work, but also naming the marginalization I've been privileged to *not* directly experience as a white, cisgender, able-bodied male.

As our conversation unfolded, I spoke plainly about the "isms"—racism, sexism, and the rest—still pervasive everywhere, including in corporate America. I discussed my Passion in righting those wrongs, supporting those directly impacted, and getting others on board to do the same. I also named the access I sometimes have, and the voice I'm afforded (oh, it can be a loud one)—that gets me heard in rooms where others aren't . . . and my commitment to use that access to open doors, not take up space.

Oh—and the energy I have to do this work—oh, I still have a TON of that!

Oh, oh—and guess what else Mr. CEO?! If you're really committed to this journey, you and I will need to be key partners—meaning I'm about to add even more to your already-full plate!

Oh, oh, oh—and guess what else?! You and I—we also BOTH need to acknowledge this thing we have called white privilege—yeah, yeah, that's the stuff I was alluding to before, and, funny story, I was actually advised to *avoid* talking about that today, but you actually just flung the door open when you shared how there have been occasions that term has been directed at you, and how it can be frustrating when some assume you haven't had to overcome things yourself, or that you "don't care" or "don't get it"—but Mr. CEO, as they say in corporate, that challenge is actually an opportunity, because if you DO care and you DO get it and you DO acknowledge certain privileges you (like me) have been granted due to nothing more than biology and you DO show them you care not through your words but through your actions, then that white privilege that YES, YOU AND I BOTH POSSESS doesn't make you a bad person at all—do you know what it means?!?! It means you (like me) have this powerful tool you didn't ask for, but it's this thing you (like me) can totally use for good—not for our own advantage but on behalf of others who don't have it, who don't hold those same levels of power and privilege that us white dudes have, and the more we understand and acknowledge these abilities we've been given based on nothing more than dumb luck . . . and the more we can link arms with others like us AND not like us, the more WE HAVE THIS INCREDIBLE ABILITY TO HELP MAKE THIS COMPANY AND THIS WORLD A BETTER PLACE!

The 20-minute call went 80 minutes. And while my Passion ran high, it ended up being matched by his. Oh, and in case you're wondering—I did take a few breathes in between all of that . . . and did a ton of listening as well.

Call #17 was the job offer.

My Passion, experience, ability to listen, and willingness to be brave, authentic, and truthful signaled that I was the leader they could trust. My readiness to take risks—with the goal of opening minds rather than shutting them down—signaled to them I could deliver the kind of meaningful impact they were seeking.

Case in point: that other term I was told to avoid—"unconscious bias"? After some time in the role, I pushed for a live training on the topic—built it, got it approved, and delivered over 60 sessions. It became the most popular and highest-rated training at the company. The CEO—aka my new "co-conspirator in inclusion"—not only gave it his stamp of approval but became one of its biggest proponents, telling everyone how much they'd personally get out of it *and* how much it supported an inclusive and high-performance culture.

Once again, I trusted myself and led authentically—and it paid off.

Leader, Know Thyself: Guiding Principles

As Firestarters—and as leaders—it helps to reflect on moments when our leadership and Courage were tested, how we responded, and the results. Over time, "guiding principles" can emerge: approaches that work for us and that we can model and share so others can refine their own style.

In the stories I shared, a handful of guiding principles kept me on my path and helped me lead with authenticity and Courage:

- Trust myself, but know I don't have all the answers.
- Be honest, but be respectful.
- Be mindful of my energy, as it'll be matched by others.
- "Calling someone out" is rarely as effective as "bringing someone in."
- Negativity is contagious, and so is Passion.

These have been steady anchors I could always return to, whether I'm coaching one person, creating a strategy with a team of 10, facilitating a workshop for 100, or speaking to a crowd of 1,000.

Your guiding principles will look different, because everyone's approach is unique. If you're using an Impact Journal, I encourage you to give consideration to what those might be.

EXERCISE: GUIDING PRINCIPLES

- Take some time to reflect on three experiences on your impact journey when your leadership and Courage were tested but you successfully pushed through.
- Identify what supported your effectiveness in those experiences—the mindsets or behaviors you feel you can continue to rely on as guiding principles in the future.
- Which principles come naturally, and which require you to lean into Courage so they keep showing up?

Capture what emerges in your Impact Journal. Keep these guiding principles close, and return to them when you're facing uncertainty or high-stakes moments.

The clearer you are on your guiding principles—and the more you trust yourself to lean into them—the more you'll ignite the meaningful impact you're meant to have, Firestarter.

REFLECTING ON ONGOING COURAGE

- What micro-moments called you to be Courageous, take risks, and trust yourself? Did any of them ignite a change reAction?
- How have you grown as a Firestarter who leads, and what does additional growth look like for you?
- What are some guiding principles that help you drive meaningful impact?
- What used to scare you but now feels doable, and what fueled that shift in Courage?
- What still scares you now, and how can you set that aside in the name of impact?

PART THREE

SUSTAINED

The Coals Keep It Burning

Don't ask what the world needs. Ask what makes you come alive, and go do that. Because what the world needs is people who have come alive.
—Howard Thurman

Toto, I've a feeling we're not in Kansas anymore.
—Dorothy, *The Wizard of Oz* (1939)

Underneath It All

Ever been heading down a path, when suddenly a big storm hits, and you rush into the safety of your home only for it to be picked up and dropped in a completely different place? Then post-storm you go outside and the farmhands have turned into a Scarecrow, Tin Man, and Cowardly Lion, and everything is suddenly in technicolor?

Okay, well, that's never happened to me either.

However, I'm guessing you've had life throw many curveballs at you. We all have. At some point we realize how little control we have over which way the universe is going to tilt on us, and what new Pulls we may experience as a result of those shifts.

Even when you have a plan in place, with your Pull-Passion-Courage seeming to be fully aligned and you thinking you know exactly where you are heading, unanticipated micro-moments can happen, often leading to macro-movements that change the trajectory of your impact journey.

But one thing is likely to remain constant: your values. These have been core heat generators—the bed of coals glowing beneath your fire. They keep your Firestarter engine running, no matter the flame's size, even through the harshest storms.

As a more experienced Firestarter, you become real clear on who you are and the values that remain core to all you do—those essential coals for your fire. So even as challenges show up that feel like they could throw you off-course, or as new sparks lure you toward what feels like a new direction, trust that your values will ground you, serve as your compass, and help you navigate turbulence on your journey.

> *Trust that your values will ground you, serve as your compass, and help you navigate turbulence on your journey.*

Keep Listening, Keep Connecting

You've heard me mention how Firestarters are often drawn to others who carry a similar fire inside.

Well, I had never met Donna Karan before writing this book, but my inner voice kept telling me to try and speak with her to understand her fire and impact journey. I knew Deborra-lee Furness was a mutual friend, so I leaned into Courage and floated the idea by Deb. Like the stars aligning, Deb helped make an introduction and Donna graciously said yes to connecting with me.

Most people know Donna Karan for the fashion empire she and her husband Stephan Weiss so brilliantly built. But what many don't know is that in 2015, she stepped away from her namesake brand to devote herself to impact work that felt urgent and essential. For Donna, this wasn't a new path—it was an evolution.

I was eager to hear her impact journey—ignited decades ago and spanning so much terrain—and to understand how she's sustained her Passion for so long, as her inner spark continues to ignite a change reAction that's now part of her legacy.

When I spoke to Donna, it was like taking a masterclass in how to honor a strong Pull, align it with Passion, and act Courageously to find solutions to real-world issues. But my biggest aha moment was when she told me how she's always approached a problem/solution situation by "connecting the dots"—a guiding principle she learned from her beloved husband and creative partner. As you may remember, this is the exact same concept discussed in chapter 2—which I had written long before I had even considered trying to connect with her. Talk about being drawn to someone with a similar fire inside.

This was a true micro-moment I'll now carry with me—proof that your inner voice deserves attention, even when it suggests something as audacious as reaching out to one of the world's most iconic fashion designers. That voice must be wired into the mysterious logic of the universe, because it's almost always onto something.

I Can't Stop at One Thing—*Donna Karan*

I've had a lot of pulls throughout my life. Loss pulled me. Love pulled me. Work pulled me. When I see problems, I see solutions—you know, it's like creation. That's just who I am.

I was born into a world of fashion, but I never thought that would be my path. My father was in fashion, my mother was in fashion, and 7th Avenue was the last place I'd ever want to be. I wanted to sing like Barbra Streisand and dance like Martha Graham—that was my dream in life. But life had other plans.

But I got pulled in—though I am not your typical fashion designer, because it's not about fashion. For me everything is about problem and solution. I just wanted to make clothes for me and my friends—women constantly moving and on the go. My father was a tailor, so I picked pieces that made sense—boom, boop, really simple and stupid. My Seven Easy Pieces that I started in 1984 are still relevant today.

Then the pulls began on my impact journey. When the AIDS epidemic broke out, it was a horror. We were losing all our friends, and I felt a calling. I went to Perry Ellis: "Perry, how do we discuss the AIDS epidemic?" He said, "Donna, this is a private issue; this is not for discussion." It freaked me out a little, and then Perry passed away.

The industry was dying and you couldn't do anything—that drove my direction. I started saying to

Anna Wintour, to Carolyne Roehm, to everyone—we've got to do something. I wanted stores where designers could dump the extra clothes, because we design far too much—too many collections, too much stuff—and let the money go to AIDS. And when Anna wants to do something, it gets done—and we started Seventh on Sale. There were three of us in the younger generation of designers—Calvin Klein, Ralph Lauren, and me . . . I was the token little kid . . . and Oscar de la Renta and Bill Blass and . . . everybody did something. That first year we raised over four million dollars. That's what I call conscious consumerism—designing with a purpose. Dressing and addressing.

Then we realized it wasn't just men dying; it was women and children, too. So we created another Seventh on Sale right by my studio, and the kids would come and paint with artisans and play games—it was extraordinary. Dress and address.

Then my girlfriend, Liz Tilberis, had ovarian cancer. The first thing we did was gather clothes and sell them at her house. I ended up doing Super Saturday in the Hamptons for ovarian cancer for almost twenty years. Again, designers would bring in their clothes, because there's always extra, and let these clothes go to a reason and a purpose. Dressing and addressing kept growing.

And my husband Stephan got ill. He was my life—the man I loved more than anything in the world. Every day he would put dots on paper, and from those dots came his sculptures, and they even became the designs for all my fragrance bottles. He passed away right before he was supposed to have his first art show, and he said to me, "Donna, whatever you do, take care of the nurses."

Now I had to connect the dots—so I went into hospitals and realized what the problems were. There needed to be more care in healthcare. With a problem, you need a solution. From that, Urban Zen Integrative Therapy was born, to combine Eastern healing modalities with Western medicine practices, and to support the nurses, doctors, patients, and their loved ones.

I'm not telling you any of this was easy—it was hard. But I've lost so many people in my life—my father when I was only three, my first boss, Anne Klein, and my mother in my 20s, my best friends, my husband . . . it is my way of handling the pain. It's selfish—but I feel good when I help people, and they inspire me.

And that's how Haiti pulled me in. I was doing work around healthcare, and President Clinton, who I had dressed, said, "You've got to go to Haiti." I believe he changed my life more than anything. The President was very involved with Haiti—he loved Haiti. And I had traveled and worked with artisans all over the world, but I didn't even know where Haiti was. Well, I went and fell in love—with the people, the artisans, everything. And I realized every single person in Haiti was an artist! Another pull: finding ways to support and preserve culture.

My three main areas of focus with Urban Zen are: the past—preservation of cultures; the present—putting the care back in healthcare; the future—educating and empowering children.

To me, it isn't about fashion—but I use fashion to connect the dots. My husband did it literally—dots to sculpture. I do it in life.

One time, a spirit spoke to me: "You have to know when to let go and move to your next stage." And right now I'm fighting with that, because my next stage has always been dressing and addressing, but if I can't do it properly and it's not working, I've got a problem.

The way of the world today—the globe is falling apart. It's probably one of the biggest fires we've ever dealt with. We have to stop and figure out how we can all come together to create a *United* States—not separated. Now, to me, this is the biggest problem we have, and this is over my head. But what I have through Urban Zen is a space and a place where people can come together to talk, in an intimate way, to see how they can solve some of these problems, and to reach out to those they know who can help.

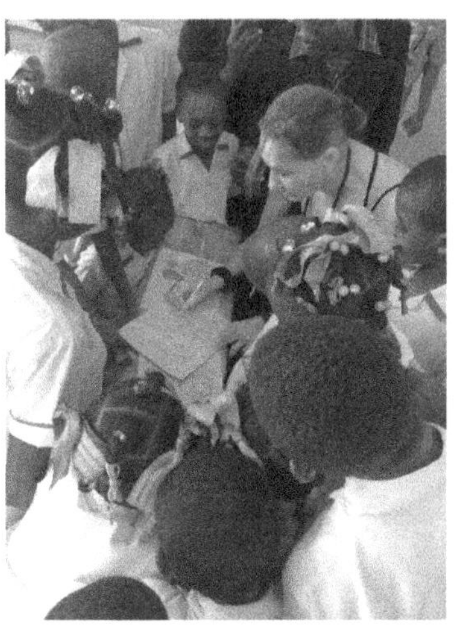

I am a "we" person, not a "me" person. And I can't stop at one thing.

So I keep refining. We can plan all we want, but we have to be in the second of the moment and the moment of the second—to be here now.

If you want to make positive change in the world, my advice is to talk to other people and find what inspires you. And use your intuition—your vision, your feeling, your soul. And be in nature. I go to rocks—I talk to rocks, I hold rocks, I do colors with rocks. People think I'm nuts—which is true—but I'll go into the park and hug a tree. Nature is a healer because it sits there, and it is there, and it talks to you. And God will talk to you.

It's not going to be a thought—it will be in your soul. You don't need to use your brain—your heart will tell you.

• • •

Shifts Can Be Seismic or Subtle

Donna's story is a prime example of how life's unanticipated micro-moments can lead to macro-movement shifts on our impact journey. It's also a reminder that much of life is outside our control—which is why listening to our hearts and trusting ourselves matters.

Sometimes the shifts that come from new Pulls aren't as macro as Donna's. I think of my friend Mimi Lemay.

My initial connection to Mimi started with me randomly reaching out—similar to what I did with Donna . . . and Greg Louganis . . . and Gregory Maguire . . . fine, fine, I see the pattern, too. (#FirestarterGroupiesUnite!) Anyhow . . .

This was 10 years ago—I had just read Mimi's incredibly moving essay, "A Letter to My Son Jacob on His 5th Birthday,"[2] and my inner voice (yet again) whispered *reach out*. I did, and a week later we were seated across from each other in a coffee shop.

In writing this book, I learned that my reaching out—and that simple coffee date we had a decade ago—became a catalytic micro-moment in *her* impact journey. It connected her with a wider circle of Firestarters and steered her toward advocacy she might not have pursued otherwise. (Didn't I tell you it's important to listen to your inner voice?!)

Over that span of time, Mimi's impact journey has remained values-aligned and kept a consistent through line, even as different needs, Pulls, and life phases have shifted her in new—yet equally meaningful—directions.

---

[2] Mimi Lemay, "A Letter to My Son Jacob on His 5th Birthday," *Boston.com*, February 26, 2015, https://www.boston.com/culture/parenting/2015/02/26/a-letter-to-my-son-jacob-on-his-5th-birthday/.

Evolving Focus, Steady Values—*Mimi Lemay*

I was raised in a hermetically sealed ultra-Orthodox community. The message that young women in the schools I went to received was that their "purpose" was auxiliary to the purpose of the man they would eventually marry. That was a challenge because I was outspoken, even passionate about things I cared about, that I saw as injustice. In my world, the things I wanted to do were frowned upon—even speaking out in front of men in my own community was off-limits. I felt unable to use my talents, abilities, or passion to affect change.

I left Orthodoxy and stopped practicing ritual Judaism at age 22 and eventually got married and had children. One of my children is transgender, and when I realized that I needed to fight for his acceptance and equal rights, I finally found the voice that I had longed to have when I was a young girl. I knew I had a story to share that was different from those most were hearing at the time: If we love, support, and make an effort to understand our trans children, they can thrive. I hoped these words would make a difference.

Years into my advocacy, I felt a different pull, and it came from realizing I could draw upon my upbringing in a very strict faith community to speak to people across various communities of faith who wanted to support trans kids but didn't know how to fit it into religious teachings. My personal experience helped me understand them, speak to that, and model the evolution that I went through.

As the years went on and my children became teenagers, I stepped back from most public forums to respect their privacy and let them tell their own stories. I shifted my energy to where I could be effective—helping parents, partnering with organizations I support, and choosing smaller, values-driven forums where my voice could bridge understanding.

Since the October 7, 2023, Hamas attacks in Israel, a new need has emerged: addressing the growing tension between parts of the Jewish community and longtime progressive institutions some no longer feel supported by. In certain instances, that fissure has directly impacted support for LGBTQ+ kids and communities. I now feel pulled toward helping bridge this divide—engaging across differences so we can keep working together for equality. I do so by honoring the pain and validating feelings of frustration or abandonment—without letting either overshadow the moral imperative to support these kids.

It's a balancing act that demands more of my intellectual focus, patience, and emotional regulation, and it asks me to use my voice to bring people into one another's lived experiences. In this season my focus is keeping the mission centered on kids while engaging in hard conversations inside my own community.

The friends and allies I have made along my impact journey keep me going, as do the young people I feel so protective of—including my own. And the values that

I strive for—justice, empathy, and equality—are the North Star I try to keep sight of, even as circumstances around me continue to shift and my focus evolves.

• • •

Values as Guardrails

Some shifts on my own impact journey have felt minor and easy to navigate, while others have felt so drastic that I questioned if I was even still on the same path.

Yet, similar to Mimi, the Pulls I followed—and the values beneath them—kept confirming I was on course. Over time, key Pulls began to emerge, and the core values that serve as guardrails for my journey crystallized:

Key Pulls		Core Value
Uplifting people	→	Dignity and belonging
Expanding access	→	Empowerment and agency
Addressing injustice	→	Equity and justice
Connecting humans	→	Collective power

That appears tightly packaged now, but in no way was all of that clear to me early on. It took years of trying things, feeling things, and noticing when my fire dimmed or roared. When my fire is fully ablaze, I know I'm living my values and serving a larger purpose.

One way I can tell if I'm off-course? I feel restless, unfulfilled, or in low spirits. This might happen because I'm not taking action toward at least one of my key Pulls, or I've landed in an environment where a core value is absent. This is when I either work to change the conditions—or realize I might need to move on.

For Firestarters, our values are essential to our existence, as they help direct our choices and set the boundaries for every step forward.

Here's how you can read the terrain and stay aligned when your journey turns rough.

Rounding a Blind Curve

Sometimes you're exactly where you want to be, living your values with your fire steadily burning, and then the rug is yanked out from under you.

In diversity, equity, and inclusion work, where much of my impact journey has focused, it's not uncommon to see an organization's commitments shift, budgets shrink, and roles disappear. You've possibly experienced similar challenges on your impact journey. It's not just a logistical nightmare—it's emotionally exhausting. It also raises questions as to whether the work was ever truly valued, or if your efforts even meant anything.

Other times tragedy can strike: a diagnosis, a loss, a global pandemic. Norms vanish, plans evaporate, life is put on pause, and it's scary as hell. There's no sugarcoating how devastating these hardships can be. But sometimes—often much later—these experiences come along with an unexpected offering: a renewed sense of purpose. It's a strange silver lining when a key Pull begins to show up in a new way, you feel your Passion begin to rise, and you find yourself connecting with a new community of changemakers.

So when things get extra hard, but you're still sensing heat inside you, this is the time to get quiet and ask: What's Pulling me now? What keeps whispering *this matters*? Which core values—the coals banked deep inside—have sustained me so far, and how will they guide my next move?

Finding a Reroute

As discussed in chapter 5, sometimes your flame begins to dim and you hit one of those WTF (where's the fire?) moments—when you simply need to find ways to add more fuel. Once you do, your fire is burning strong again.

But that might not always be the case. You might have gotten to the point where it feels like no amount of fuel additives will cut it—the Passion in your heart appears snuffed out.

It can be hard to admit when the flame is just about gone—because you still care, your values haven't changed, and the issues you've been working on remain. But for whatever reason, you might just no longer be feeling that strong Pull or Passion.

This doesn't make you inhumane; it makes you human. It doesn't mean you're no longer a Firestarter; it means to get a fire going again, you'll need some new sparks. Sometimes you're just ready for something new, which means there's an opportunity to use your changemaker skills, values, and Passion somewhere else.

If you notice your flame staying consistently low, then it's a good time to grab your Impact Journal and take a "spark inventory."

EXERCISE: SPARK INVENTORY

Find a quiet space and spend some time reflecting:

- On a scale of 1–10, where does your longstanding spark land right now? Why did you give it that rating?
- What aspects of your journey have made your spark brighter vs. dimmed it?
- If your Pull from before isn't Pulling anymore, do you sense a new one coming on? If not, what sparks—old or new—still have your attention?
- Even if you feel off-track on your impact journey, do you still feel that Firestarter spirit calling you to make a meaningful impact?
- What values have been the "bed of coals" under your fire all along—and how can they serve as a steady compass as you look ahead?

Step back and notice what this spark inventory reveals about where things stand right now—and whether change may be on the horizon. Based on this insight, consider what deserves your attention next.

One thing is for sure: You can't force a flame. Give it air and time. With your strong values banked like coals, the heat will hold until your fire reignites or new sparks appear. Your flame will rise again when it's meant to.

Breathing Through Toxic Air

Values don't only guide the path forward; they can also signal when it might be time to exit.

Occasionally you might find yourself in a situation where things get so ugly you have to choose: stay or go—for your own good. The reasons can vary: breached values, a hostile environment, unsafe conditions, crossed integrity lines, contaminated culture, or unrealistic expectations. It might feel like a tough decision, but toxic air is going to harm you and can choke out your fire—so the healthiest move is often to remove yourself from the situation.

During one phase of my journey, I was brought into a corporate organization where I was offered an opportunity to do work I loved and lead toward real impact. The problem was, the person who called the shots was so demeaning that I (and other colleagues) spiraled into a state of anxiety and depression. It got so bad that I knew, for my own good, I had to walk away. The experience twisted my perspective and did so much damage to me *and* my fire that I thought I might never step foot in a corporate environment again. Fortunately, because I got out before an irrecoverable amount of damage was done, those wounds were able to heal over time. That allowed me to give corporate a chance again, and I've had many healthy, rewarding, and values-aligned experiences since.

Navigating Strong Headwinds

Sometimes external forces can hit so hard that it feels as if a storm has torn everything apart or flipped it completely upside down. This can bring everything, including long-held values, into question.

I have recently experienced this on my own journey due to the unprecedented surge of coordinated efforts to completely discredit and dismantle "DEI."

It's important to recognize that DEI stands for three virtuous words: diversity, equity, and inclusion. For over two decades, this has been the umbrella term for the work I've done and am so proud of. It's also what I see as a metaphorical umbrella—offering protection from systems and practices that too often marginalize, exclude, or devalue people.

For me, diversity, equity, and inclusion work has been a calling that tied together my key Pulls: uplifting people, expanding access, addressing injustice, and connecting humans. These are ideals I would hope most people can get behind, and they have been the foundation of my efforts to make this world a better place. That is why I've found so much gratification and success in the work—and why the recent backlash against DEI has felt so painful.

With that said, I do understand why some recoil when DEI work is done . . . for lack of a better word . . . wrong.

If executed poorly, it can take shape in ways that almost guarantee failure. When it shows up as box-checking or performative gestures, it becomes insincere. When it's done in a shaming or retributive way, it becomes divisive. When it's designed in a way where some have to lose in order for others to gain, it becomes a zero-sum strategy. With flawed approaches, no one wins.

But if executed well, diversity, equity, and inclusion work can create environments where everyone feels valued, respected, and has the opportunity to thrive.

This work is nuanced and delicate. When it's done wrong, just like anything else, pushback is understandable and the approach should be reexamined and adjusted. But when it's done right, you can clearly feel people coming closer together, not being pushed further apart.

With all of that said, I'm now going to ask my inner-Pollyanna to step aside for a moment so I can call something out: not all of the backlash is due to flawed implementation. A good deal of the pushback also stems from discomfort with change, fear of losing power, a lack of empathy, and a whole bunch of -isms and phobias rearing their ugly heads. As history has shown us time and time again, progress propels pushback.

Because of all these factors (and I'm sure many more I haven't named), we've recently seen decades' worth of hard-won gains rolled back almost overnight. The headwinds have been strong and quite difficult to navigate.

So I've had to ask myself: Do I have the Passion to keep going? Or do I get out for my own good? Is it time to scrub my résumé, create a new LinkedIn account, and start over because my past roles now read (to some) like scarlet letters?

I'm right around the age when I'm supposed to be having a midlife crisis, but instead I'm suddenly having an existential one!? (Kidding . . . kind of.)

Leaving a toxic organization to keep my fire lit and just doing similar work somewhere else was a "no brainer." Even the Scarecrow would have known that was the right move.

But being pushed away from my Pull—that's different. Those coals beneath the surface of my fire—my values—are still generating a ton of heat. The impact I've always strived for—bringing people together and making this world a better place—feels needed now more than ever.

It's a confusing time and the future is uncertain, but there's one thing I know for sure: No one gets to choose my next move but me.

Change is inevitable, and staying committed as a Firestarter, especially through the storms, is damn hard. When possible, it can be helpful to try to reframe a challenge as an opportunity in disguise. (Growth mindset!) Or as the Scarecrow said in the *Wizard of Oz*, "It's not *what* you see, but *how* you see it that makes all the difference."

And remember: When the path ahead is unknown, even in the more advanced stage of your impact journey, stay laser-focused on your values and keep pivoting in the way that feels right to you. Just make sure you're always heading toward the heat.

Permission to Pivot

Once upon a time, you **emerged** as a Firestarter. You poured your heart into the work, which resulted in meaningful and **ongoing** impact. It eventually got to the point where others started turning to you, looking for guidance and leadership. So how could you now even consider going in a different direction?

Because shift happen.

No matter how long you've been on your journey, new Pulls can emerge, expanding both possibility and impact. Yes, it can be hard to accept that one chapter might be winding down—even if a new one is beginning to write itself. But as a **sustained** Firestarter, you know yourself far better now—your values, motivations, and how you can be most effective as a leader and catalyst for change.

> *Your purpose today might be different from what it was in the past and what it might end up being in the future.*

You might find yourself thinking, "But wait . . . wasn't *that* my purpose?" I don't believe our purpose is ever necessarily just one thing. Nor do I think we should put pressure on ourselves to "figure out our purpose"—and then feel locked into it for the rest of our lives. Your purpose *today* might be different from what it was in the *past* and what it might end up being in the *future*.

Everything you've done up until this point has mattered, and the impact you set in motion will continue through a change reAction. So now, if something new is whispering *look over here, this matters, too*—it's okay to listen. It's okay to explore. It's okay to pivot. You may be needed in other ways you don't even realize yet.

Give yourself permission to evolve and adapt. As long as you're aligned with your key Pulls and core values—and following your heart—you can't go wrong.

Key Pulls and Core Values

If you could use some assistance clarifying your key Pulls and core values, here's an exercise you can complete in your Impact Journal to help.

EXERCISE: KEY PULLS AND CORE VALUES

Step 1—Spot the Sparks

Write down 3-5 memorable moments when you were part of something bigger than yourself—times you knew you were doing something that truly mattered and could feel the impact in motion.

Step 2—List the Actions

Next to each moment, list the actions you took (speaking up, creating, supporting someone, organizing, etc.).

Step 3—List the Objectives

Ask yourself: *What was I hoping to achieve through those actions?* The answers will reveal your Pulls—your underlying objectives or motivations.

Examples:

Action		**Objective (Pull)**
Supporting someone	→	Uplifting people
Building a program	→	Expanding access
Speaking up	→	Addressing injustice
Organizing a group	→	Connecting humans

Step 4—Identify Your Key Pulls

Do any Pulls show up multiple times or feel more important than others? Those are your through lines or where you're feeling the most heat—your key Pulls.

Step 5—Identify Your Core Values

For each key Pull, ask: *What value does this represent for me?* These values are the steady coals that keep your fire alive, even when the flame shifts.

Examples:

Key Pull		**Core Value**
Uplifting people	→	Dignity and belonging
Expanding access	→	Empowerment and agency
Addressing injustice	→	Equity and justice
Connecting humans	→	Collective power

REFLECTING ON SUSTAINED PULL

- When life has thrown a curveball at your impact journey, what core values have felt important to hold onto?
- If your impact journey lands you in a situation that feels toxic, how will you know when it's time to step away to protect your fire?
- Do your key Pulls today feel the same as they did earlier in your journey? Are any new Pulls emerging?
- Have you felt a sense of purpose at different points in your life? Do you have a sense of what it might be right now?
- Do you plan to keep heading in the same direction, or might there be a shift in the path ahead?

Want to see a clip from Tom's conversation with Donna Karan?

Scan the QR Code below or visit
www.thenextlevelimpact.com/firestarter-videos

Protect the Flame

Caring for myself is not self-indulgence,
it is self-preservation, and that is an act of political warfare.
—Audre Lorde

You're capable of more than you know.
—Glinda, *Oz the Great and Powerful* (2013)

Tending to Your Own Needs

You've been on this journey long enough to know you never know what's coming. Some days are smooth and steady with clear skies. Others are hit with harsh storms or unexpected danger. Despite the unpredictability, you have every intention to keep going, though you realize that will require your mind, body, and soul to stay aligned and in peak condition if you want to make it for the long haul.

At this stage, even the seemingly basic things can make a big difference. Maintaining a balanced pace helps you avoid burning out. Having people who support you provides stability and strength when the path gets unsteady. Keeping your tank full—physically, emotionally, and spiritually—ensures your inner flame has the fuel to carry you further for longer.

But no one else is going to be monitoring your fuel level close enough to know when you're running dangerously low. Nor will anyone else realize when a thorn in your side needs to be removed before it causes a serious infection. And those dark clouds that sometimes form above, which others might see but you are much more aware of? Well, it's on *you* to decide if it's time to momentarily step off the path and take shelter.

Because you are wired to think about the common good, there's a strong chance you spend more time tending to everyone else's needs than your own. And while that's damn admirable, if you get caught in the storm, stumble on the rocks, or let your engine burn out, you'll be sidelined—unable to help anyone else, including yourself.

You are capable of so much, but that doesn't make you invincible. If you want to sustain yourself and this journey for the long haul, you'll have to make some very intentional choices to keep your flame protected and your fire burning—because we don't want your journey to end before it's meant to.

Well-Being Essentials

My impact journey has had plenty of bumps, storms, and twisty turns—possibly just like yours. I don't have it all figured out. Far from it.

Here's the truth: Every "best practice" I now use to protect my flame has come from times I dropped the ball on taking care of myself—and I learned the hard way. As time moves on, and as I get further along on my journey, the stakes feel higher, and even my own mortality doesn't feel theoretical anymore. I'm finally realizing that there are some well-being essentials that are critical when it comes to longevity. I've found the most important ones to be nurturing our **b**odies, finding **b**alance, setting **b**oundaries, and leaning on our **b**uddies. Think of these as your vitamin **B**s—essential for maintaining your energy.

I always knew those essentials mattered, but *emerging Firestarter Tom* didn't fully grasp just how much. Now I do—because energy is finite for all of us, and the work we care about requires a steady flame, not a burnout bonfire.

Here's a breakdown of those four well-being essentials that shouldn't be overlooked:

Body

Who loves a delicious pizza and extra-strong margarita? Me! Who finally realized (years later) it was time to cut back? Sigh . . . me again (womp womp). Sure, those things give me a quick hit of joy and stress relief, but it is always short-lived—and the weight gain, sluggishness, and overall blah feeling added up.

I'm no medical doctor, but I know this: What I put in my body—and how I treat my body—affects almost everything for me, physically and mentally. Food and alcohol. Sleep (which, yes, gets trickier with age). Movement—stretching, walking, actual workouts. It's easy to let days (even weeks) slip by without giving much thought to any of it. When I treat my body better, it pays off. When I don't, I pay for it.

I've also had to pay closer attention to my mental health. I could only find myself randomly bursting into tears in the middle of a grocery store so many times before saying, "I think I need some help." The more we're expected to *have our $h!+ together*, the harder it is to admit when we're struggling. But I've learned that the sooner I speak up—and actually address it—the sooner I find myself in a better place.

I've had to make self-care a priority. My perspective shifted from "let my fire go full blaze for as long as possible" to realizing that approach only leads to burnout. The more energy, clarity, and stamina I have, the greater the impact I can make.

A Firestarter's self-care routine doesn't have to be perfect—mine certainly isn't. But it does have to be intentional.

→ Protect your body. Protect your capacity.

Balance

As a parent, I find myself stressing the importance of balance to my kids all the time . . . like not overdoing it with junk food, screen time, or staying up too late. In doing so, I've become much more aware of what I'm modeling for them in my own life and actions. This has pushed me to be far more intentional about practicing what I preach when it comes to this aspect of protecting my Firestarter flame.

Day-to-day life already demands so much from us—work, family, friends, responsibilities, hobbies, personal/professional development, etc. As if that's not enough, you've also got that dang internal voice continuously ringing in your ear *this matters . . . do something . . . if not you, then who?!*

Well, Firestarter, I'm sure in many ways you're a hero—but you're not a superhero. (Still human!) Life's balance gets out of whack all the time, and it's important to recognize when that's happened and do the work to get rebalanced. For instance, in recent years, my "sandwich caregiving" responsibilities—caring for both my children and aging relatives—have often felt logistically and emotionally overwhelming. None of life's other responsibilities have gone away, and that's made it even harder to prioritize my health, work, sleep, other relationships, and—oh yeah—my impact journey.

Sometimes that's just reality; there isn't always a big fix. But there are almost always small moves that can be made toward balance. I might push myself to take a walk, check in with a friend, or power off the screen and get more rest. And as for that fire in me to "make this world a better place, in my own unique way"? Sometimes I have to honor it—but then say, "Not right now. I've got other things to focus on." (Every once in a while, that even means focusing on myself.)

→ Energy is finite. Balance it wisely.

Boundaries

For us empaths, boundaries can be very difficult to put in place—we're wired to put others first. But if we want the stamina to have impact where it matters most, setting appropriate boundaries is essential to protect our flame.

If you pay close attention, you'll start to notice your *fuel additives* versus *energy drains* (you may have identified some in chapter 5's Firestarter Check-Up). Those drains can come from other people—or from our own behaviors. This is where boundaries become some of the strongest protectors of your flame. It's your right to say: "No," "Not now," "That doesn't work for me," or "This needs to end."

In the spirit of kindness, I try to do this without being abrasive. However, I've realized that sometimes firmness is required—especially when dealing with long-standing patterns or people with strong personalities who don't "hear you" setting that boundary the first (or third) time. One goal I have when setting a boundary is doing it in a way I won't regret or feel ashamed of later. If the words I used were made visible for others to see, would I stand by them as a justifiable form of self-protection (as opposed to unkindness)? If yes, then I'm good.

I've had to give myself permission to sit with the discomfort—and even the unintended hurt—that boundaries can create. It's hard, but when someone or something consistently has a negative impact on me, I've learned I deserve to stand up for myself just like I would for someone else.

If you're working on this, get clear on your *What-Why-What*: *What* is creating the problem? *Why* does it need to stop? *What* does "good" look like? Once you're sure of those answers, stay grounded in them, explain them to whoever needs to hear them, and then get back to what matters—without getting bogged down in the unnecessary.

I've also had to set self-imposed boundaries. A recent one has been around my news and social media intake. It's become so clear to me how continuous negativity across various information platforms brings me down and puts me in a headspace that's anything but productive. Setting personal limits around this has been very important for my well-being. I'm not burying my head in the sand (though some days I'd like to), but in a 24/7 news cycle where you can scroll for hours and barely see anything positive, I've realized I have to put personal boundaries in place so I can stay in the game longer.

→ Boundaries keep you grounded, focused, and fueled.

Buddies

The final crucial component of protecting your flame is having the support of others. It's essential to have people you can lean on when things get tough: friends, family, colleagues, health and wellness providers, and whoever else helps you stay steady.

I've turned to people I'm connected to from all over the map (many in this book) when I've gone through hard times, searched for answers, or wanted to dream big. It's helped me feel less alone, sparked new ideas, and given me the push I've needed to keep going—or turn in a new direction.

There's real power in having support from those directly connected to your impact work *and* those with no affiliation, who are simply there for *you*. Lean on your people in the good times and the hard times.

→ Buddies fuel endurance—don't carry the fire alone.

Making It Through the Storm

Even the most capable among us can find ourselves caught in situations we never imagined. This makes me think of my friend Darcy Bouzeos.

I've known Darcy for more than half my life, and she is one of the strongest and smartest people I know. That's what makes her story so striking to me. Grasping the storm she made it through—and the path it sent her down on her impact journey—has been incredibly inspiring. Her story is a powerful reminder of the unimaginable turns life can take, what those experiences can lead us to, and the importance of protecting ourselves and our flame.

Protecting What Kept Me Going—*Darcy Bouzeos*

For me, protecting the flame meant pausing my volunteer work when my spirit was being depleted so I could continue offering hope without losing myself.

I had endured years of verbal, emotional, and psychological abuse in my marriage. After five difficult years, I finally found the strength to extract myself from that relationship. It was one of the most painful experiences of my life, but over time, I began to heal and move forward. As I came to understand more about the insidious nature of covert abuse, I felt a powerful calling to help other women who were trapped in similar situations.

My passion for this work was amplified by a deep awareness of how fortunate I was. Yes, I had endured horrific behavior from my now ex-husband, but I also had financial resources through my business, a strong network of loving family and friends, and—perhaps most significantly—I didn't have children with him, which so often keeps women tethered to their abusers.

I began volunteering at a facility for abused women and eventually joined the Board of Directors. Witnessing the gratitude and transformation of women as they "connected the dots" of the harm they had endured and began to rebuild their lives was profoundly moving. Their courage inspired me to deepen my commitment.

When I moved to California, I found a church where a few insightful pastors recognized how pervasive covert abuse is—particularly among women of faith. They gave me the opportunity to build something meaningful: an entire ministry dedicated to supporting women experiencing or recovering from emotional, verbal, and psychological harm in intimate relationships. From that ministry grew a weekly support group that, over the years, served hundreds of women.

Once a woman truly understands what was done to her in a covertly abusive relationship, she can never "unsee" it. That moment of clarity often marks the beginning of real healing. There is incredible power in recognizing that a partner intentionally sought to control and diminish you. With that awareness, women learn, grow, and ultimately thrive once they break free from those toxic bonds.

But after ten years of serving in this space, I began to feel the weight of it. Bearing witness to so much pain and trauma can be profoundly draining. I knew that if I didn't protect my own light, I wouldn't be able to offer hope to anyone else. So, I made the difficult but necessary decision to step back. I still don't know if—or when—I'll return to that work in a formal way, but I understood that my well-being had to come first.

Right now, my focus is on restoring my own hope—particularly around love and relationships—and believing that a healthy, kind, and emotionally safe man can still be part of my future.

Even as I step back, my heart remains tethered to this mission. I continue to read, learn, and counsel women one-on-one, offering guidance, support, and resources to help them begin their journey of understanding. I've developed an ability to recognize when a woman is trapped in a covertly abusive relationship—whether she's a friend, a colleague, or even a stranger in the grocery store. Helping a woman name what's happening to her is profoundly rewarding, because awareness is always the first step toward freedom.

I am, admittedly, not the person most people would expect to have been caught in an abusive relationship. I've always been confident, strong-willed, and outspoken against injustice. That's precisely what makes my story so important. Covert abuse can touch any woman. I believe God allowed me to walk through that dark season because He knew I would use it to help others find hope and healing.

When people walk through tragedy or trauma, many feel a deep desire to reach back and help others. It's a beautiful transformation—one born of empathy, compassion, and purpose. I believe God plants that desire in us, calling us to walk alongside others so that, together, we can bring light, hope, and healing to places where it's needed most.

• • •

Sparks of Wisdom

Darcy's journey not only teaches us about resilience and impact, but also how to transform a dark season into a positive change reAction that lives on through every life it touches.

It wasn't until I was nearing the end of assembling this book that a common thread jumped out at me: Every fire that burned inside of the contributors had its origins in hardship, pain, or injustice. I'm guessing that is not a coincidence, but more likely a very common trigger for this whole Firestarter-thing.

That said, there's a good chance this might be the case for *your* fire, as well. For that reason alone, I want to take a moment to offer love, peace, and gratitude to every Firestarter out there—because we deserve it.

Another common thread: Every Firestarter in this book who's been on their journey for a while and still has that fire in them takes "protecting their flame" very seriously. And clearly that's an important thing to do, because we Firestarters have been through a lot.

Don't be fooled into thinking that taking care of yourself . . . is a luxury. It's actually a strategic necessity. Longevity depends on self-preservation.

Please don't be fooled into thinking that taking care of yourself—or even (gasp!) putting yourself first—is a luxury. It's actually a strategic necessity. Longevity depends on self-preservation.

Don't just take it from me. Here are some insights from Firestarters whose stories you've already come to know, aligned with the well-being essentials mentioned earlier:

Body

- *I know, for nurturers, we're always taking care of everyone else and leaving ourselves till last. We can't neglect ourselves. I know I have to self-care. I'm realizing now that it is so important—I have to make sure that I'm good.*
  —Deborra-lee Furness

- *Especially now . . . with how difficult things have gotten . . . I still care just as much, if not more, but I've realized I need to take care of myself in the process as well.*
  —Jazz Jennings

- *I take care of myself. I go to the gym. I get a massage. I'm always working on my mental health.*
  —Jeanette Jennings

- *Don't be afraid to take a step back and take care of yourself.*
  —Raffi Freedman-Gurspan

Balance

- *It's very useful to remind yourself to slow down. Sometimes I have to take myself off to a room and sit and be conscientious about what life is requesting of me, and how I can address the needs of the moment, given the skills that I have and the energy and focus that I have.*
  —Gregory Maguire

- *Having a relationship and family was, and still is, very important to me. The work-life balance, especially in advocacy, is tough to maintain.*
  —Raffi Freedman-Gurspan

- *I'm in this space now where I feel like what I have owns me and I don't own it, so I'm wanting to shed everything to discover who I am.*
  —Greg Louganis

- *It is so important that we have joy in our life because we need that for our well-being.*
  —Deborra-lee Furness

Boundaries

- *In this season of life, I've learned to say no, and I've learned what I bring to the table in terms of value and worth.*
  —Sherri Shepherd

- *I left the job. I ended the relationship. I walked away from the house. And I chose myself for the first time.*
  —Wendy Pollack

- *I've learned that people-pleasing is not good for you or the other person—you end up resenting the person.*
  —Deborra-lee Furness

- *I have had to draw boundaries and honor myself by knowing my limits . . . that's something that took a while to learn.*
  —Raffi Freedman-Gurspan

- *I made the decision to stop . . . I knew I needed to take a break . . . it was affecting my spirit.*
  —Darcy Bouzeos

- Social Media/Technology:
  - *You can read comments and go down the rabbit hole, so I have to step away from that, distance myself from it.*
    —Jeanette Jennings
  - *I'd rather scrupulously stay away from social media.*
    —Gregory Maguire
  - *The addiction to phones is one of our biggest problems . . . throw away the phones! Get off the computer!*
    —Donna Karan

Buddies

- *Talk with others who understand the importance of what you're doing. Run alongside others fuelled by a similar mission.*
  —Renée Leigh

- *In those moments when strangers' voices echo the lies my inner critic already whispers, I lean on my friends and allies. Without that circle of support, I would have let imposter syndrome stop me a hundred times over. And never be too proud to ask for help!*
  —Mason Dunn

- *What helps me stay fueled and connected to myself, especially when the pressure gets heavy or the path feels long, is the unwavering love and support of my family and closest friends. They are my anchor. When I'm feeling weighed down by doubt or questioning whether I'm doing enough, they remind me of my worth and the impact I've already made. They celebrate my victories, no matter how small, and hold me up when I feel like I'm falling. Their belief in me rekindles my own belief in myself, and that love fuels my purpose. It keeps me moving forward, even on the hardest days.*

—Jazz Jennings

We Can't Have You Burn Out

The journey might feel long, but our time on earth is short.

If your Pull is still strong and your Passion still burns within, let's keep that going in a healthy and sustainable way—because we don't want you, or your fire, to burn out before it's meant to.

Just as you show up for others, show up for yourself. Listen to your body. Do your best to keep life as balanced as possible. Know when to say no. Lean on those who care for you as much as you care for them. I hope those types of people are abundant in your life. And if not, I encourage you to find ways to connect with other Firestarters to help change that.

REFLECTING ON SUSTAINED PASSION

- How can you tell when your flame is running low?
- Which of the well-being essentials—body, balance, boundaries, and buddies—are you strongest in right now, and which one needs the most attention?
- When have you not practiced self-care when you should have, and what did it cost you?
- Who in your life helps you protect your flame rather than dim it—and how can you strengthen those connections?

Sustaining your fire is easier when surrounded by others who get it.

Visit www.thenextlevelimpact.com/resources or scan the QR code below to learn about the Firestarter Community, a simple way for readers of *It Lit a Fire* to stay connected and inspired on the journey.

The Fire Lives On

People now ask me if I'm passing the torch.
I always explain that no, I'm keeping my torch, thank you
very much. And I'm using it to light the torches of others.
—Gloria Steinem

Read what my medal says: "Courage."
Ain't it the truth? Ain't it the truth?
—Cowardly Lion, *The Wizard of Oz* (1939)

You've Never Walked Alone

> *Your impact doesn't end when your pace softens—it lives on in the fires you've lit along the way.*

Every journey has an arc. And yes, it's often said that everything has a beginning and an end. But is that always true? What if some things are meant to live on?

I want you, Firestarter, to see your journey not as one with a fixed endpoint, but as one that endures—not just because of what you've done, but because of the change reAction your spark has ignited.

Your impact doesn't end when your pace softens—it lives on in the fires you've sparked along the way. Your Pull, Passion, and Courage are part of something far bigger than one lifetime.

At some point, you'll begin to slow down. But remember—you haven't walked this path alone. You've also been lighting the torches of others along the way. It's okay to step aside and let someone else begin to lead—with fresh eyes, steady hands, and plenty of fuel still burning—and carry the fire forward.

One day, you may need to hand off your torch entirely and step off the path. That's okay, too. Before you do, take a moment to look back. You'll see your footprints—still visible. These are marking the way for others who are continuing on their own journey, walking in the warmth of the fire you helped ignite.

Eventually, you'll rise from the earth and into the skies above. But even then, your presence will remain. Those still walking below will feel you with them—watching with great pride, fires still ablaze.

You care deeply, and you are not alone. You are part of the strong Firestarter community—and together, our fires create something powerful and enduring.

Impact Spreading Like Wildfire

It was over 20 years ago that Dr. Ronni Sanlo first sensed a spark in me and set my fire ablaze when she invited me to do my assistantship at the UCLA LGBT Campus Resource Center. I had no idea how much she would serve as a guide for me, or how profoundly she would alter the trajectory of my life.

The more I got to know this fierce Firestarter—nearly three decades older and almost a foot shorter than me (yet somehow still larger than life)—the more I realized she's one of the bravest people I've ever met. Her Passion and Courage have always been contagious, rubbing off on me and countless others. She is simultaneously creating change *and* lighting fires wherever she goes—it's as though she's an *impact multiplier*, continuously setting off change reActions.

To this day, Ronni remains both a mentor and a friend. I aspire to show up for others the way she has always shown up for me.

Isn't That What It's All About?— *Dr. Ronni Sanlo*

As an 11-year-old Jewish girl growing up in North Miami Beach in the 1950s, I knew I was a lesbian when I fell in love with Annette Funicello . . . the best Mouseketeer EVER! But I stuffed away my sexual identity for 20 years, causing a lifelong struggle with PTSD. I finally stopped lying to myself and others and came out at the age of 31, when my truth emerged . . .

It was 1979 in Florida, two years after anti-gay Anita Bryant began her national hate campaign. During my divorce hearing, the judge invoked Bryant's name and took away custody of my children—they were three and six. It was the worst, most impactful event of my life and it kickstarted an anger that moved me from "nice mommy lady" to "militant homosexual." Though my children and I reunited when they were in their twenties, the pain of loss had created a fiery passion for me to be present for other young people. I knew that fire would never leave me because it was truly a matter of survival. Still is . . . and I'm 78 years old. If I let the fire die, I'd die.

My impact journey began when I started just saying "yes." **I said yes** when the Florida Lesbian and Gay Task Force needed a director in 1981. **I said yes** when I was asked if I wanted to work in the Florida AIDS program in 1987. **I said yes** when I accepted free graduate school admission as a work perk in 1989. **I said yes** when the University of Michigan offered me a position to direct the Lesbian and Gay Men's Program Office in 1994. **I said yes** because I believed that things would get better for LGBTQ+ people as long as we showed up, spoke out, and did the work.

The pain I carried was sometimes more than I could bear—I had attempted suicide three times. But I must have a survival gene somewhere inside of me because I kept doing the work, despite always being afraid—over and over, all the way to today.

I believe I've had the biggest impact because of the way I've protected, loved, taught, and transformed LGBTQ+ college students. And my legacy to higher education is Lavender Graduation, which I created in 1995 to honor the lives, scholastic achievements, and unique gifts of LGBTQ+ students. It's the event that tells them that they mattered to the institution.

The only thing that made me step away from this glorious work was retirement. But the reason I retired when I did was because I had become too distant from college students. I was in my mid-60s, an old-time lesbian activist who at that point had very little in common with the students I was supposed to serve. I realized that my responsibility was to step out of the way and let the younger, smarter higher ed professionals—those I taught—continue the work. My vision for the work had been met. My role needed to become that of a mentor, a cheerleader for those who would carry on what I started years ago.

At age 78, my fire has never waned. I remain lit by the current political situation, fearing for the lives of my children and grandchildren, fearing for LGBTQ+ people and, frankly, for myself and my wife as old lesbians. But my impact journey most certainly isn't over. I have begun an organization called the Lavender Graduation Legacy Project which supports Lavender Graduations both in high schools and with community organizations who wish to host Lavender Graduations for older LGBTQ+ people who didn't have Lav Grad.

Today, my fire is lit, one day at a time, as I write about my life and try to make the world safe for people yet again. My bigger overall purpose is to wake up, show up, speak out, and live as large and loud as I'm able. I am blessed to receive messages from former students almost daily with words of thanks, love, and appreciation—and that keeps me inspired. If they can move forward with courage and a loving heart, I can, too—and isn't that really what it's all about?

• • •

On the Shoulders of Giants

The saying couldn't be more true for me: I stand on the shoulders of giants.

It's only because of people like Dr. Ronni Sanlo, Greg Louganis, Deborra-lee Furness, and other incredibly Courageous heroes who paved the way that I can now have my own impact journey. I am so blessed to get to follow in the footsteps of some of these greats.

The same might be true for you. For so many of us, our impact journeys are only possible because of those who came before us as well as those who have inspired us along the way.

> *It's so important to live every day like it counts—and to never take the Firestarters in our lives for granted.*

What an honor to realize that, one day, others will say the same about us. That's the change reAction.

The truth is, none of us can ever fully grasp who our impact is reaching—or what life has in store for us. That's why it's so important to live every day like it counts—and to never take the Firestarters in our lives for granted.

A Legacy Like No Other—*Tim and Stacy Wakefield*

Tim and Stacy Wakefield came into my life in a completely unexpected way. My husband Jimmy and I had been invited to attend an overseas event for Home Base, a program established and run by the Boston Red Sox Foundation and Massachusetts General Hospital. Home Base provides free, comprehensive care for the invisible wounds of war for veterans, service members, and their families.

I decided to bring a baseball along on this trip, hoping to possibly get some signatures on it for our son. At the airport, a fellow traveler heard my plan with the ball and said, "Tim Wakefield and his wife Stacy are seated right over there; they're such nice people and that would be an amazing signature to get!"

Transparency time: Jimmy and I were clueless when it came to baseball. But that wasn't going to stop me, so over I went . . . and minutes later I had my first signature secured and had indeed just interacted with two extremely nice people.

As fate would have it, an hour later I was seated next to Tim and Stacy—30,000 feet above ground on a seven-hour flight "across the pond." Sometimes an internal spark is ignited by other people—and that ended up being the case for me with these two instant friends. Beyond just learning he was a former baseball player, I didn't know (or care) who the heck Tim was from a notoriety standpoint. All I knew was that he and his wife Stacy exuded a kindness that was impossible to miss. Plus, Tim was wearing a fantastically big and funky ring with a "B" on it that Tom **B**ourdon was determined to get a selfie with (mission accomplished!)—and maybe talk Tim into lending me long-term (no such luck).

Tom flashing one of Tim's championship rings.

Okay, how the heck was I supposed to know that was one of his two World Series Championship rings? Or that he was one of only a few renowned knuckleballers in MLB history? Or that he holds countless records—including being the oldest active MLB player when he retired, after 17 years with the Red Sox (and 19 in the league) at age 45? I know that stuff really matters to a lot of people. But I'll be honest—it was all the other stuff

I learned about Tim and Stacy that made them both champions in my mind.

Tim's impact work has truly spanned the gamut. He was the Red Sox's first Dana-Farber Cancer Institute Jimmy Fund Captain, supporting cancer care and research. He helped launch Home Base, supporting veterans, and served as its Honorary Chairman.[3] He created the "Wakefield Warriors" program, bringing hospital patients to Fenway Park to spend time with him and watch batting practice before home games.[4] He started a celebrity golf tournament that raised over $10 million for the Space Coast Early Intervention Center, a preschool program for children with special needs.[5] He served as the Honorary Chairman of the Red Sox Foundation for a full decade. He was an eight-time nominee and eventual winner of MLB's Roberto Clemente Award—presented to the player who best reflects the spirit of giving back to the community. And the list goes on and on.

From left: Tom, Tim, Stacy, and Jimmy.

And that drive toward compassion and impact ran in the family. Stacy and their two children were right there

[3] Maria Stephanos, "Red Sox Tim Wakefield's Legacy: How an idea led to the founding of Home Base," *WCVB.com*, November 10, 2023, https://www.wcvb.com/article/red-sox-tim-wakefields-legacy-founding-of-home-base/45793655.

[4] Gayle Fee, "Ex-Sox hurler Tim Wakefield a charity ace," *Boston Herald*, May 27, 2015, https://www.bostonherald.com/2015/05/27/ex-sox-hurler-tim-wakefield-a-charity-ace/.

[5] Red Sox Foundation, "Honor Tim Wakefield's Legacy," RedSoxFoundation.org, October 3, 2023, https://www.redsoxfoundation.org/uncategorized/honor-tim-wakefields-legacy/.

alongside Tim for so many of the efforts—such as raising funds for pediatric cancer charities and showing up year after year as a family to deliver Christmas presents to children in hospitals.[6]

I would have loved nothing more than to speak with my friends directly as I wrote this book—especially for this final chapter, where I have the honor of uplifting their extraordinary impact journeys. But heartbreakingly, the universe tilted in a shockingly unexpected direction and made that impossible.

On October 1, 2023, Tim passed away at age 57, soon after a brain cancer diagnosis. Only two months after losing him, Stacy kept the tradition going, returning for their annual visit to the children's hospital to bring Christmas presents to young cancer patients—even as cancer was advancing in her own body. On February 28, 2024, Stacy passed away at age 53.

It's unexplainable—how something like this could happen so suddenly, and to such beautiful souls.

The impact of their lives—and their passing—was felt deeply by people across the world. The tributes poured in from every corner, all echoing the same truth: Tim and Stacy Wakefield made this world a better place.

> *Tim's kindness and indomitable spirit were as legendary as his knuckleball. . . . He had a remarkable ability to uplift, inspire . . . the true definition of greatness.*
>
> —John Henry
>
> Principal Owner, Boston Red Sox[7]

---

[6] Phil Tenser, "Stacy Wakefield, widow of Red Sox pitcher Tim Wakefield, dies after cancer battle," WCVB.com, https://www.wcvb.com/article/stacy-wakefield-obituary-boston-red-sox/60010664.

[7] Red Sox Foundation, "Honor Tim Wakefield's Legacy."

It's one thing to be an outstanding athlete; it's another to be an extraordinary human being. Tim was both.

—Tom Werner
Chairman, Boston Red Sox

Tim exemplified every humanitarian quality in the dictionary . . . I can only aspire to live as genuinely and honorably as he did.

—Sam Kennedy
President and CEO, Boston Red Sox

He did so much for charity and didn't ask for cameras to show up. He did it for all the right reasons.

—Derek Lowe
Tim's longtime teammate[8]

To a lot of people [Stacy] was Tim's wife, but to us she was definitely her own powerhouse.

—Lisa Scherber
Director of Patient and Family Programs,
Dana Farber's Jimmy Fund Clinic[9]

We will remember Stacy as a strong, loving, thoughtful and kind person, who was as down-to-earth as they come.

—Family statement[10]

---

[8] Anna Lazarus Caplan, "Tim and Stacy Wakefield Honored After Their Death at Red Sox Game as Their Daughter Throws Out First Pitch," *People*, April 9, 2024, https://people.com/tim-stacy-wakefield-honored-at-red-sox-game-daughter-throws-first-pitch-8629226.

[9] Kyle Hightower, "Stacy Wakefield had a passion for service that continued after husband Tim Wakefield's death," AP News.com, Updated February 29, 2024, https://apnews.com/article/stacy-tim-wakefield-red-sox-b8df25a201904eba27adf8d2bb9211f9.

[10] Boston Red Sox Media Relations, "Statement from the family of Stacy Wakefield," Boston Red Sox, February 28, 2024, www.mlb.com/redsox/press-release/press-release-statement-from-the-family-of-stacy-wakefield.

Tim and Stacy's passing—still heavy on the hearts of anyone who knew them—left me with three lasting reminders I now carry forward:

1. When good people come into your life, appreciate them as much as possible, for it's a gift like no other.
2. Live your life in such a way that when you're gone, people will say: "You made this world a better place."
3. A Firestarter's impact doesn't disappear when they're no longer here. Their legacy continues to burn brightly, carried forward by those they've inspired.

As for the third point, it warms my heart and gives me a strong sense of peace knowing that Tim and Stacy's children—now young adults—continue to walk in their parents' footsteps. The deep commitment and internal fire to help others has been passed on in a beautiful change reAction, carrying Tim and Stacy's legacy forward with grace and purpose.

• • •

E Ala E—Awaken. Arise. Rise Up!

It had been a rough six months leading up to me writing this book.

My job leading diversity, equity, and inclusion for a global company had been discontinued. The entire field of DEI had come under attack. I was caught squarely in the sandwich-caregiver role, with massive pressures and responsibilities compounding all at once from fatherhood, the needs and major health issues of my aging parents, and my beloved 97-year-old grandmother entering the final stage of her journey.

The emotional weight of juggling disruption and loss on multiple levels was more than I expected.

The universe must've known I was in need—not just of a break, but of a spark. In a completely random turn of events, Jimmy and I were invited to something called the Maui Songwriters Festival. We had no idea what it was, and leaving behind the chaos at home—even for a week—felt irresponsible, if not impossible. But we knew how much we could use the respite. So we called in a few favors, rallied support, and somehow were on our way to Hawaii.

When we got there we were immediately surrounded by beauty and serenity in every way possible. On our second morning, we headed to the ocean long before sunrise to attend something we had been invited to called *E Ala E*—a Hawaiian call to awaken, arise, and rise up.

We didn't know what to expect, we had merely been told it was an incredibly spiritual experience led by a Native Hawaiian elder. Before we knew it, we were floating in the ocean as light began to break through the darkness. We were surrounded by about 20 others, and some of them—including Yvonne Mann, who you met in Chapter 2—became forces of light for us that week and beyond.

After the sun had fully peaked over the horizon, we quietly gathered and formed a circle on the beach. The elder slowly approached each of us, one at a time, gently placing his forehead to ours—standing in momentary silence, connected, one human to another.

The sacred gesture made time feel suspended, anchoring me in a moment of deep connection—with the universe, and with humanity.

After the ceremony culminated, Jimmy and I gathered our belongings and began to quietly walk away. As we passed the elder—who was speaking with a few others—I made quick eye contact with him and silently muttered, "Thank you."

We kept walking, but then I heard him call out: "Excuse me?" I turned around and he asked if he could speak with me for a moment.

I took a few steps in his direction, and he said he had sensed a strong energy in me. That's why he'd called me back.

Then he asked, "Could I have your hands?" We had gone from forehead to forehead . . . to now holding hands? What was happening!?

I placed my hands in his, and although only seconds passed, it felt as if time stood still once again.

Then he looked directly in my eyes. "There is a **fire** in you."

*There is a **fire** in you.*

Tears began to stream down my face.

It was as though he looked right into my soul. He couldn't have been more right. There *is* a fire in me. But it had never been explicitly identified as such—by me or by anyone else—until that very moment.

In my earlier stages of life, I didn't even know it was there, probably because it was still forming—by all the experiences I had to go through first, including those key micro-moments that created the big sparks.

It truly started burning in those early UCLA LGBT Campus Resource Center days. Since then, there have definitely been times when it has waned—but by continuing to add fuel, it always came back full force.

But there have also been some darker periods, where it dimmed to the point that I questioned if my fire still existed . . . or whether it really even mattered . . . or if I would ever have a fire in me again. And in the months leading up to writing this book, I was in one of those darker periods. I didn't know if I had any Pull, Passion, or Courage left in me. And even if I did still have a spark of Firestarter spirit remaining, was I up for yet another sharp (and this time, blind) turn in my journey?

I had been scared and lost—aware that no one else could give me the answers I needed. At best, they were buried somewhere inside of me. At worst, I'd only uncover them by taking Courageous risks . . . not knowing if I was still on the right path, or about to crash and burn.

Then suddenly, this gentle elder got quiet with me, somehow made time stand still, looked deep into my soul and reminded me: There is a fire inside of me that I am not meant to ignore.

Even though I felt like I was in the dark, I had to summon Courage and figure out where my path was leading me next. Maybe not all that different from what I had been doing all these years.

And I had to stop questioning whether my fire needed my attention. Or if I was having any impact. Or if I was living my purpose.

Of course.

Of course.

Of course.

As educator Brené Brown suggests in her book *Braving the Wilderness*, this would mean standing in my own wilderness—vulnerable, potentially alone, but true to myself—with a sense of true belonging.[11] This would require believing I am exactly where I am meant to be, and who I am meant to be.

---

[11] Brené Brown, *Braving the Wilderness* (Random House, 2017).

Or per my own mantra: I needed to trust in myself.

Since that experience, I've done my best to set fear aside, be Courageous, and stay open to wherever my path will now take me—heart wide open for change.

I've spent quite a bit of time reflecting on my personal impact journey, which I've come to realize is such a core element of my very identity. Since the beginning, my Pull and Passion have centered around creating spaces where people can show up fully, be seen for the brilliance they carry, feel empowered, and thrive.

But as I looked closer, another pattern began to emerge—one that felt just as essential. I've had the privilege of fueling the flames in others—supporting the growth of changemakers at all levels, increasingly so over time. Through both formal and informal teaching, coaching, and mentorship, I've had the privilege of helping others navigate their own journeys, uncover their own answers, and step into their own power. In fact, some of my most meaningful experiences have come from this part of my journey—especially as I've watched the impact ripple outward.

Just like when the light broke through the darkness as I floated in the Maui ocean, I could suddenly see what was in front of me as this new direction in my path revealed itself. Similar to my mentor Ronni, I too have the ability to be an *impact multiplier*—helping ignite the fire in others so they can create meaningful change in their own way.

Now, my continued Passion and *new* Pull have aligned. With this clarity, my own fire is once again roaring.

Of course, the annoying voice of self-doubt keeps piping in . . . *"Wow, Tom . . . you sure have some big kahunas to come back from Hawaii and suddenly think you're meant to be some kind of Firestarter of Firestarters."*

Well, then—big kahunas it is. I'm leaning into Courage, the third essential element of the Firestarter equation, and honoring my inner voice calling me in that direction. Following in Ronni's footsteps yet again—**I said yes**.

There is a fire in me. I am a Firestarter.

I will acknowledge my Pull, follow my Passion, and let Courage rise up to meet any fear or doubt that tries to get in the way. I will do my part to make this world a better place, in my own unique way.

And there is a fire in you. You are a Firestarter.

Acknowledge your Pull, follow your Passion, and let Courage rise up to meet any fear or doubt that tries to get in the way. Do your part to make this world a better place, in your own unique way.

E Ala E—Awaken, arise, and rise up, Firestarter.

REFLECTING ON SUSTAINED COURAGE

- How will you acknowledge your Pull, follow your Passion, and let Courage rise up to meet any fear or doubt that tries to get in the way?
- How will you do your part to make this world a better place, in your own unique way?
- How can you be a Firestarter of Firestarters?
- How do you want to be remembered in terms of the impact you've had?

Conclusion: You Lit a Fire

You always had the power, my dear.
You just had to learn it for yourself.
—Glinda, *The Wizard of Oz* (1939)

We can't let good be just a word. It has to mean something.
—Elphaba, *Wicked: For Good* (2025)

Nowhere Near Finished

As this book comes to an end, your journey is likely nowhere near finished.

Something lit a fire in you. I can't encourage you enough to honor it, be proud of it, and use it to create meaningful change while helping others light their fires.

It might sound cliché, but now, more than ever, we need as many Firestarters out there as possible—doing what they can to make this world a better place. Even when it feels like divisiveness has peaked and the world is coming apart, I'm certain there are millions of us who want to come together, support each other, and focus on the greater good.

I am so grateful to the contributors in this book, who were gracious enough to share their time and stories with me so I could share them with you. These Firestarters inspire me and fill my heart with warmth—as do the countless other Firestarters in my life whose stories aren't included here but whose impact is just as significant.

I'm also grateful to all of you Firestarters I have not yet had the honor of meeting—I truly hope our paths cross one day. Whether you are in the emerging, ongoing, or sustained stage of your journey, we all have so much to learn from one another. And as large as this world (and Firestarter community) is, there are countless ways to connect and uplift each other. Let's commit to that, because there is incredible strength in numbers.

I thought I'd close with one final Firestarter story—that of my friend and colleague, Jennifer Brown. Jennifer is a true gem; she stepped into the world of diversity, equity, and inclusion about five years before my own impact journey began in that space. She has wowed, supported, and inspired me—along with thousands of others—through her dynamic personality, books, keynote addresses, and consulting agency that I was fortunate to be part of for a number of years. Jennifer has a truly special way of helping people imagine what a better world can look like—and how each of us can play a part in getting there.

Transformation Never Stops—*Jennifer Brown*

In my twenties, I moved to New York to become an opera singer. It was thrilling, a life built around beauty, connection, and the power of the human voice—but a few years in, I injured mine. Surgery repaired the physical damage, but emotionally I was shattered. Singing had not just been what I did—it was who I was, but it seemed that journey had ended.

In the quiet that followed, I thought I had lost my way. But that silence had something to teach me. When I finally stopped clinging to the identity of "singer," space opened for something else to come through. I began to sense a quiet pull and was guided, slowly and unexpectedly, in a new direction: leadership development. I discovered, to my surprise, a whole new kind of stage.

Working with leaders and teams in the corporate space, I felt the passion again—this time with what enables humans to thrive together in systems. I realized my purpose had been less about performance and more about voice—expression, belonging, and helping leaders find the courage to use their own. My journey had not ended; it was simply changing form.

The word "voice" continued to carry deep meaning for me. As a queer woman, I had been in and out of the closet, both in the arts and later in corporate settings. Losing my literal voice, then reclaiming it, mirrored the process of finding and owning my authentic one. My calling had evolved into helping others—especially those long silenced or sidelined, to speak their truth and be heard.

Eventually, I founded my own firm focused on inclusion, belonging, equity, and amplifying voices that had been silenced for far too long. For two decades I have had the privilege of working with leaders, teams, and organizations—inviting them to bring more voices to the table, listen more deeply, and lead with courage and care. My pull, passion, and courage had aligned—and I was now inviting others to do the same.

But if life has taught me anything, it is that transformation never stops asking for us. The same way that my singing voice once failed me, the world around us now feels like it is straining through backlash, exhaustion, and fear. The path forward is not clear.

And yet, I have come to believe this moment, like that earlier loss of my singing voice, is not an ending—it's a season of renewal, where we must tend the ground so new growth can take root. What looks like contraction is also incubation. The systems we have built are under strain, but as we see happen in nature, I believe they are actually composting—and this is where regeneration begins.

I'm reminding myself, and others, to pause, breathe, and trust the cycles. The new is born through some letting go, but the foundation underneath it all—our values that serve as underlying coals to keep our fire burning—will endure.

As my story keeps rewriting itself, I'm constantly reminded that every version still requires the same instrument: my voice. And every experience any of us has had—every triumph, heartbreak, and reinvention—becomes raw material for what's next.

We are all between worlds right now—between what was and what is coming. That in-between space is uncomfortable, but it is also holy ground. It is where we are asked to lean into courage, use our voices, and take action to make this world a better place.

Wherever you are on your journey, keep following your pull, fueling your passion, and choosing courage. And keep in mind one of the most important lessons I've learned on my own impact journey: The voice always finds its way back.

• • •

Stay Committed, Stay Connected

Thank you for going on this journey with me.

It is my hope that *It Lit a Fire* has inspired you—and sparked new ideas—as you keep striving to make this world a better place, in your own unique way.

Keep using your Impact Journal to capture the sparks you sense in yourself and in others; the Pulls that whisper *this matters—do something*; the Passion that helps you follow the heat; the times you choose Courage to strike the match; the micro-moments that build into macro-movements; and the values that keep you on track. If you're up for sharing via social media, let us be part of your impact journey by including #ItLitAFire in your post.

Stay committed to honoring your Pull, following your Passion, and choosing Courage.

Trust in yourself.

And finally, remember this, Firestarter: You don't need to have it all figured out—none of us do. Nor do you have to boil the ocean . . . at least not all at once! Focus on what's right in front of you, because every action is meaningful. Even changing one life for the better is change that matters—and it can ignite a change reAction that lives on forever.

It Lit a Fire

Continue the Journey: Additional Resources

The journey doesn't end here.

Whether you're reading *It Lit a Fire* on your own, wanting to process the content as a group, or ready to put the Firestarter Model to work with your team, you can access additional resources to support ongoing learning, real-world action, and connection with fellow Firestarters.

Visit www.thenextlevelimpact.com/resources or scan the QR code below to access guides, prompts, community spaces, and opportunities to take the next step—together.

Acknowledgments

I am beyond grateful to so many incredible people in my life who helped make this book possible.

To my husband, Jimmy: Thank you for being there for me, supporting me, keeping me balanced, making me laugh, driving me a little batty—and letting me do the same for you. You complete me, and I am so lucky to have you.

To our children, Lukas and Maya: You are my everything. I want to be a better human and make this world a better place because of you. Dad and Baba love you more than you'll ever know.

To my parents, Jerry and Kay, and my sister, Sarah: I am so blessed to have grown up with three caring, kind, compassionate souls who love and support me unconditionally. Thank you.

To my wonderful network of friends: I am so lucky to have so many great people in my life—too many to name individually, but please know how much you all mean to me.

To the contributors of *It Lit a Fire*: Words cannot express how grateful I am for your contributions to this book. I asked for your participation because of your heart, the way you see the world, the impact you have, and your ability to inspire others—including me. The fact that you said "yes"—and let me keep coming back with additional asks—says everything about the kind of people you are. The legacy you are building is profound, and it's my honor to have captured even a small snapshot of it in these pages. Keep that flame burning bright.

To the Publish Your Purpose team: I can't thank you enough for your support and for helping me bring this book to life. A special shout-out to Jenn Grace for the amazing, impact-focused company you've built and to Alex Loutsenko for being the steady guide behind the scenes, keeping me organized, grounded, and supported every step of the way.

To the Spark Squad: Thank you for helping me launch *It Lit a Fire* into the world!

To the millions of Firestarters out there (some I've met, most I haven't . . . yet): I am eternally grateful for who you are and what you do to make this world a better place. Even when things feel hard, remember that you play an essential role in your community, school, company, nonprofit, faith network, circle of friends, and family—and that what you do truly matters. Let's keep finding new ways to connect and support each other. Take care and keep going—onward and upward.

Photography Credits

In order of appearance. Any images and photographs not listed are from the author's or contributor's personal collection.

Gregory Maguire

Page 15: © Helen Maguire Newman. Used with permission.

Greg Louganis

Page 51: courtesy Greg Louganis.

Page 52: credit Greg Gorman. Used with permission.

Jeanette Jennings

Pages 72–75: courtesy of Jeanette Jennings. Used with permission.

Mason Dunn

Page 80: credit Chris Hurley. Used with permission.

Raffi Freedman-Gurspan

Page 88: credit Raffi Freedman-Gurspan. Used with permission.

Deborra-lee Furness

Page 92: credit Michele Aboud. Used with permission.

Jazz Jennings

Pages 103–105: courtesy of Jeanette Jennings. Used with permission.

Donna Karan

Page 124: credit Luca Babini. Used with permission.

Page 127: credit Russell James. Used with permission.

Ronni Sanlo

Pages 161–162: courtesy of Ronni Sanlo. Used with permission.

Tim & Stacy Wakefield

Pages 165–166: from Tom's personal collection.

E Ala E

Pages 170–174: credit Nicki Fletcher. Used with permission.

Tom Bourdon

Page 189 & Back cover: credit Adam Waz. Used with permission.

About the Author

Dr. Tom Bourdon is a sought-after trainer, coach, consultant, and facilitator who helps individuals and organizations create meaningful change in the world.

A leadership, inclusion, and impact strategist, he is the founder and principal of Next Level Impact, launched in 2025 to partner with people and organizations ready to turn their values into action.

Tom previously served as a Diversity, Equity, and Inclusion leader at Staples and BigCommerce; led Greater Boston PFLAG; and directed LGBTQ+ centers at UCLA and Tufts University, where he also helped launch the Social Justice Leadership Initiative. He has partnered with numerous organizations, including Google, Microsoft, and Hasbro, to strengthen inclusive leadership and drive meaningful organizational impact.

Tom received his doctorate in Organizational Leadership from Northeastern University, his master's in Education from UCLA, and his bachelor's in Business Administration from Babson College. He has been a certified coach for nearly 20 years and holds active credentials through both the International Coaching Federation (ICF) and the Board Certified Coach (BCC) program.

Known for his compassionate style, authentic energy, and thought-provoking approach, Tom is a frequent keynote speaker and moderator on leadership, inclusion, and purpose-driven change. He lives in Massachusetts with his husband and their two children.

Connect with Tom

Website: www.tombourdon.com
LinkedIn: www.linkedin.com/in/tom-bourdon
Instagram: www.instagram.com/drtombourdon
YouTube: www.youtube.com/@tombourdon

www.linktr.ee/thenextlevelimpact

Work with Tom

Through Next Level Impact, Tom Bourdon provides coaching, keynotes, training experiences, and strategic advisory support for individuals, leaders, teams, and organizations who want to create change that actually sticks. Drawing on more than two decades of work in leadership, inclusion, and impact, Tom helps clients cut through the noise, get clear on what matters most, and move forward with practical, real-world action aligned with their values.

Whether you're an individual looking to clarify your purpose, navigate a transition, or expand your impact, or an organization aiming to strengthen inclusive leadership, build a healthier culture, and advance strategic priorities, Tom serves as a grounded thought partner and trusted guide.

Visit Next Level Impact online or connect with Tom on social media for support that meets you where you are and helps you get to where you want to go.

Connect with Next Level Impact

Website: www.thenextlevelimpact.com
LinkedIn: www.linkedin.com/company/thenextlevelimpact
Instagram: www.instagram.com/thenextlevelimpact
Facebook: www.facebook.com/thenextlevelimpact

https://linktr.ee/thenextlevelimpact

Next Level
Impact

The B Corp Movement

Dear reader,

Thank you for reading this book and joining the Publish Your Purpose community! You are joining a special group of people who aim to make the world a better place.

What's Publish Your Purpose About?

Our mission is to elevate the voices often excluded from traditional publishing. We intentionally seek out authors and storytellers with diverse backgrounds, life experiences, and unique perspectives to publish books that will make an impact in the world.

Beyond our books, we are focused on tangible, action-based change. As a woman- and LGBTQ+-owned company, we are committed to reducing inequality, lowering levels of poverty, creating a healthier environment, building stronger communities, and creating high-quality jobs with dignity and purpose.

As a Certified B Corporation, we use business as a force for good. We join a community of mission-driven companies building a more equitable, inclusive, and sustainable global economy. B Corporations must meet high standards of transparency, social and environmental performance, and accountability as determined by the nonprofit B Lab. The certification process is rigorous and ongoing (with a recertification requirement every three years).

How Do We Do This?

We intentionally partner with socially and economically disadvantaged businesses that meet our sustainability goals. We embrace and encourage our authors and employee's differences in race, age, color, disability, ethnicity, family or marital status, gender identity or expression, language, national origin, physical and mental ability, political affiliation, religion, sexual orientation, socio-economic status, veteran status, and other characteristics that make them unique.

Community is at the heart of everything we do—from our writing and publishing programs to contributing to social enterprise nonprofits like reSET (https://www.resetco.org/) and our work in founding B Local Connecticut.

We are endlessly grateful to our authors, readers, and local community for being the driving force behind the equitable and sustainable world we are building together.

To connect with us online, or publish with us,
visit us at www.publishyourpurpose.com.

Elevating Your Voice,

Jenn T. Grace

Jenn T. Grace

Founder, Publish Your Purpose